MW00331390

FINANCES FOR TEENS

BY

STEVEN TYLOR O'CONNOR

DIGITAL Fabulists

los angeles

Published in the USA by
Digital Fabulists
11684 Ventura Blvd #205
Studio City, CA 91604
www.digitalfabulists.com

ISBN-10: 0692218971
ISBN-13: 978-0692218976

Cover graphic by Billy Frank Alexander Design

Printed in the United States of America

Table of Contents

1
Introduction

I'm going to be honest with you. This book is different than every book on finances out there. This is not the same old financial advice book that your parents might have, and it certainly isn't written by the same people. Any book that may try and address our concerns as young adults falls short. It's hard for people who already have their lives in order to remember what it's like to live paycheck to paycheck because you can only work part time because of school. This book is written for young adults by a young adult.

Nobody knows nothin'

"Nobody knows nothin'" is the mantra of a mentor of mine. Take my advice, take Suze Orman's advice, take any professional's advice, and then mesh it all together and create a financial lifestyle that works for you. It's about catering the information to fit your lifestyle, your goals and your personality.

There is a general lack of everyday, basic, financial knowledge out in the world. My goal with this book is to help you build a strong financial foundation by giving you a better understanding of finances as simply as I can. With Internet and financial talk shows inundating you with information it can be overwhelming. You may not have heard my advice before. If you have, sometimes it helps to hear the same thing in a slightly different way before it makes sense or causes us to act.

Being a young adult comes with many exciting milestones: driver's license, first job, prom, graduation, voting, and financial independence. Your first step in the world of banking is to get a checking account. When opening your first account you need to consider many factors. Finding an account that fits your style and preferences is vital. Secondly you want to build yourself some semblance of a back-up fund. I disagree with some financial experts who believe that we should focus on paying down our debt before putting money away and saving. Their logic is that the interest rate is higher on debt than in savings, so you lose money by paying more in interest on loans than you earn in interest on savings. I think you need to have SOME sort of back-up plan, no matter the amount.

For example, all through high school, I worked. I used direct deposit, so my employer put the majority of my paycheck (roughly 75%) into my savings; the remaining funds went to my checking. Since I didn't have too many bills at the time, I was able to save most of my money. As I gradually had more bills to pay, the percentage shifted, but I always kept saving. By the time I graduated and moved to New York City, I had saved over $8,000.00.

I continued to work while in school in New York. Because I was able to work hard and save wisely, I stretched my funds to last while establishing myself in the city. I rarely went into my savings account, but when I did, it was for valid reasons. My savings helped to buy a new computer when my old one crashed, buy a bed, and put a security deposit down on an apartment. It even helped pay for rent after I lost my job in an economic downturn and I couldn't find a new one. Being an adult can be hard, but if you plan ahead, you can make it suck a little less.

If I had spent all of my saved up money on paying down debt, as some experts suggest, I would have been screwed when I got into a financial jam and needed that money. Perfect example: to move into an apartment you need all of the money for a security deposit—plus an additional amount worth at least one month's rent—before you move in. So, you need all that money in addition to the money for your monthly bills. Fortunately, I had money saved up to pay for things like that.

Another important step is establishing your credit. Our economic system values people with credit. My stepfather always paid for everything in cash and never got a credit card. He believed that if he couldn't pay for it outright, he couldn't afford it. It was a good mentality, but unfortunately, when he went to buy his first house he didn't have sufficient credit to get a mortgage. His father had to co-sign and guarantee the mortgage. The point? You need to have credit so you can achieve the goals you want to accomplish in life, both short-term and long-term. I recommend getting a student credit card and building a healthy credit history and credit score.

The greatest investment you can make in your entire lifetime is your education. When you head to college you will most likely go into student loan debt. Instead of having an anxiety attack because every month you will make a loan payment for the same amount as a new Chanel wallet or X-Box, think of it as an investment.

Always keep an eye out on what is happening with the economy. If interest rates are being reduced, then you might be able to consolidate your debt into a lower interest rate. For example, if your loan is fixed at 8.5% and you can find a loan that is fixed at 5% for the life of the loan, then you should apply for the loan with a lower interest. The lower the interest rate, the less money you are spending paying the bank back, meaning more money in your pocket. Your goal should be to make consistent, on-time payments and have a loan with the lowest possible interest rate.

If you can manage, you need to start thinking about retirement. I know, it's over 40 years away, but that didn't stop me from enrolling in my 401(k) plan at Bank of America at age 16. Putting a little bit away now in my 401(k)—and then when I left the bank, into my Roth IRA—is proving that doing a little bit now reaps big rewards later. Time is an ally in banking. The longer your money has to compound, the better off you'll be.

In the following pages I will give you the tools you need to make smart financial decisions. It's possible to party in college and still be a responsible adult. Promise.

I wrote this book to pass on what I've learned in order to help. My goal is to educate you about the world of banking and personal finance, dispel any rumors or myths, correct any misinformation, and provide financial guidance. I can give you the tools necessary to make informed financial decisions.

2
Note to the Parents

IT'S HARD TO SEE YOUR CHILDREN GROWING UP. One day they'll leave the nest—if they haven't already. There is so much to worry about after they're gone, too. Are they eating properly? Are they safe? And there is just so much you want to do for them. You want to see them off to school; you want to help them clean their room, and you still want to be part of their daily lives. That day is going to be one of the hardest moments in your life because, at some point, you have to cut the strings. You have to let your children spread their wings and fly.

If you want to be a part of your child's life every single day, then leave them with a gift that keeps giving. Give them knowledge with this book so they can start making sound financial decisions. Every time your son or daughter makes a financial decision it will be a "thank you" for the solid advice you have given them. If you instill in them discipline and respect for money, your child will be able to handle the responsibilities of having money and being an adult.

You need to lead by example and provide guidance to your son or daughter. A person's financial behavior is influenced by their earliest experiences, and the manner in which those in the home deal with money sets the tone. If you handle money like it grows on trees, without planning or preparing for your bills and future, then your kids might pick up these bad habits. If you teach your kids fiscal responsibility starting from a young age, then progressively get more involved as they grow up and mature, you can leave a lasting impression on your children.

This book is perfect for your child, but it's also perfect for you. Are you aware of how building the foundation to financial success affects you? If not, you should read this book along with your son or daughter and discuss how any missteps you may have taken could have been corrected had you had the knowledge. You can also reinforce the book's teachings by explaining how doing what is recommended is sensible and useful in practice.

Whether you are reading it yourself or passing it on as a gift, you are holding a book that will help change how people think about their finances.

3
Maturing into Money

I STARTED MY FIRST JOB WHILE IN MY SOPHOMORE YEAR IN HIGH SCHOOL. A local restaurant hired me as a bus boy. At 16 years old, I was paying for car insurance every month, providing my own lunch money out of earnings, and saving money. I kept $20 in cash on me at all times and deposited the rest of my tips into my checking account. Once I had enough money in my checking for bills and some spending cash, I deposited the remainder of my income into my savings account.

My first time

The first purchase I made out of my savings was an iPod. I bought a green iPod Mini with a quotation engraved on the back. "Act Well Your Part, Therein All Honor Lies." Purchases like this one were special to me because they were the fruits of my labor.

Having to pay for my own car insurance and gas, I took care of my car and watched how I drove. Since I paid for my own lunch, I didn't waste my precious funds on junk food and snacks every day. And since I paid for my iPod, I took great care of it. That iPod lasted me over seven years until it stopped holding battery life.

I eventually changed jobs and started working at Bank of America where I stayed employed from the summer before junior year of high school until second semester of my first year in college. I enrolled in direct deposit immediately upon being hired and placed the majority of my funds into my savings account. My reasoning was that if I wasn't going to be using the funds, I might as well earn interest on the money. As I grew older and had to start paying for repairs on the car, prom, homecoming, and a cell phone bill, I slowly changed the percentage of my direct deposit to shift more money into checking to cover the costs of adulthood. As soon as I was eligible, I enrolled in my 401(k) plan where I not only put money towards retirement, but Bank of America matched my donations, giving me more money for my own retirement! Who can turn down free money?

I applied for and received my first credit card the day I turned 18. I applied for a basic credit card with no perks through Bank of America. I decided to only put gas and other small purchases on my credit card, whereas everything else I would pay with my debit card. Since I wasn't receiving any points for my purchases, there was no motivation to charge my purchase except to build credit. Every month I paid my credit card bill down to about $10 and let the $10 accrue interest.

I was not given an allowance for chores; we all pitched in on all tasks around the house because a family is a team. When we did come across money on birthdays or holidays, there was an ardent rule: you must save at least half of it. From an early age, my parents instilled in me the necessity to save. That rule has stayed with me ever since.

As we grow up, we have to make a conscious effort to continue to save. I feel like everyone should have a reason or a goal they are saving for. In my case, it was saving for an iPod, then a laptop and other college supplies, and then I began to save to have a safety net in New York City.

As long as you aren't constantly late on your bills, overdrawn on your account, or maxed out on your credit card, I give you permission to make your own financial savings goals. Want to save for this season's hottest pair of Coach boots? Go for it! Want to save up for a snowboard and equipment? Knock yourself out! Whatever you want to spend your money on, you should be able to do so; after all, you are the one who worked for that money. I am not here to tell you what to do with your money. You are the one working in a boring survival job until you can make your dreams come true. If splurging on yourself and taking a weekend trip somewhere with friends makes you happy, then do it. Life is too short to be consumed by stress and financial woes. It's just money; it comes and goes. Get this straight—I am not giving you free reign to start charging your credit card out the wazoo and get yourself so drowned in debt that your goal will have to be to pay off your debt. But if you are in control of your finances, by all means, have some fun!

First Job? Congrats!

You made the first step to being an adult! Now that you have entered the work force, prepare for a long stay. Unless you are lucky enough to win the lottery, plan on working in some capacity until you retire. Want to retire early? Well, make the right choices now, and that might just be possible.

When you get hired, you will be asked to fill out a W4 form. This is a tax form that helps gauge how much money the IRS will take out of your paycheck for taxes. Follow the prompts or ask HR personnel for help on how to fill out the W4 form.

After you've filled out your W4 form, you can now start getting paid. I recommend you enroll in direct deposit, as it is the easiest way to get paid. Ask your employer if they offer it and If they do, then you need to enroll. Direct deposit is an electronic deposit into your account by your employer. Enroll and never worry about having to rush to the bank to deposit your check.

I have a friend, Janice, who absolutely will *not* enroll in direct deposit. She claims she is afraid the government will take her money before it reaches her account. That is illegal and ridiculous. The amount of money she has paid in overdraft fees is astronomical. To be honest, $1 is too much to pay. Please, don't be like Janice. She "forgets" to deposit her paycheck then spends money she doesn't have.

After enrolling in direct deposit, look into your company's benefits. Benefits are a nice perk to the dull and boring life of working a job. Some benefits to look into are:
- Health Insurance
- Paid Time Off
- Retirement Accounts

Health Insurance- As long as you are enrolled in school, you should be covered by your parents' health insurance. So, if you have the opportunity to enroll in health care coverage, you may not want to take it. You would just be throwing away money since you already have insurance. If you don't have health insurance through your parents, then you should get it. Because if you aren't healthy, then you aren't going to be spending your money on what you want, you're spending it on astronomical health bills. Take care of yourself so you can spend your money on purchases you want.

Paid Time Off- Many jobs offer their full time (and sometimes part time) employees paid time off. This allows people to take time off from work for vacation or for days they are sick and still be able to get paid. If you are working part-time you may not receive this benefit, so you should definitely check with your human resources department about this.

Retirement Accounts- The most important benefit or perk you need to look into is if your employer offers a retirement account, such as a 401(k). If you are able to enroll in your company's 401(k), you need to do it. Privately owned restaurants and mom-and-pop shops usually don't offer a 401(k), but if you work for any kind of chain or corporation, they should offer one. A 401(k) is an account where money is deposited into it directly out of your paycheck, before taxes are taken out.

A 401(k) got its name from where the tax law is written, which is in paragraph 401, section k. I will explain why getting some form of a retirement account is important, later on in the book.

I know that retirement is decades away, but when saving, time is your friend. I am not going to give you examples with actual figures as to how much money you can earn in interest, do some research online. Furthermore, there are other books that are more in-depth and can give you better information than I can. Look online for books on this topic, or read one of Suze Orman's books. She is a great financial source, and her information on retirement accounts and their tax benefits and loopholes is outstanding. I'm just giving you advice in a nutshell.

Once you get into the habit of saving 5-15% of your gross pay now, through market fluctuations and compound interest, you can really save a hefty nest egg for your retirement. Trust me, you won't really miss the 5% out of your paycheck anyway.

If you are enrolled in a 401(k), the money will be taken out of your paycheck, which means less money for you to spend. The reason you should enroll is because 401(k) money is taken out of your paycheck before taxes are. Once the 401(k) is taken out, then you will be taxed on your new gross pay total, which means you pay LESS in taxes than if you didn't contribute to a 401(k). This is why a 401(k) is crucial to saving money for retirement. Your money is invested, pre-tax, and grows tax-free. You are only taxed when you take money out of the account when you retire. I will give you an example of how you save money on taxes.

Let's say your gross income is $1,000 per paycheck and you get paid twice a month. Now let's say your tax rate is 10%. If you do not have a 401(k), after the $100 in taxes is taken out, your net pay will be $900. Now let's say you do have a 401(k) and your deposit amount is 5% of every paycheck. Of your $1,000 gross pay, $50 will go to your 401(k), $95 will go to taxes and your net pay will be $855. Your tax burden, or the amount of money you owe the government, was reduced by $5. That doesn't seem like a lot of money, but in one year that totals to an extra $120. Over 40 years, it totals an extra $4,800 that you have saved. Of course, the more money you make, the more of a benefit this will become.

One perk to the 401(k) account is that many companies will match your contribution, but the amount of how much they match varies. When I worked at Bank of America, they matched my contributions at 100% up to the first 5%; so I contributed 5% of my pay. In the example above, 5% is $50. If your company matches at 100% for the first 5%, then on top of your $50 contribution, your company will put in $50. So, in a one pay period, you have put in $100 towards your retirement.

Just a quick note… You can only put money into a 401(k) when you are enrolled in one through an employer. Once you leave that job, you can no longer place money into the account. It will still be active and will still grow, but no more deposits can be placed into it. If you wish to continue saving (which I highly recommend) for retirement, get an IRA. An IRA is essentially a self-sponsored 401(k) that you fund yourself with money out of your paycheck *after* taxes. Once you set up an IRA, you can either roll your old 401(k) into your new IRA to consolidate your retirement accounts or you can leave them separate.

If you start putting money away now, through the returns you get on your investments over the long run and with compound interest, your money will grow into a great nest egg for retirement. I know it may hard to think about giving up some money now and putting it towards your retirement, but it will be the best decision you will ever make in your life other than going to college. Besides, if the money is taken out of your paycheck before you see it in your hand, then you won't really miss it. It's amazing how easily you will learn to cope.

Pay Stubs

When you get your paycheck, you receive a pay stub. The pay stub will have pertinent information about you and the company on it, as well as the breakdown of how much money went to taxes and how much your take home pay will be. One important number to pay attention to is your gross pay. Your gross pay will show how much money you earned for that pay period before taxes are taken out. Your taxes will be shown by telling you what you are being taxed for and how much. Another important thing listed on your pay stub will be your net pay. Net pay is the amount of money you get to take home, after taxes and deductions.

Why?

I am the kind of person who likes to know why we should do things. Why invest in a 401(k)? The answer is because it will help pave the way for your retirement. I've had my 401(k) since I was eligible to enroll when I was 16. What 16-year-old do you know has a 401(k)? In the end, it comes down to the fact that you should just do it! Just enroll and contribute. In 40 or more years, you will be glad you did.

If you leave your company, you can roll over your 401(k) into a traditional IRA, then convert it into a Roth IRA. This is my recommendation. You can only contribute to a 401(k) through an employer, but an IRA can be done through you. If you would like more information on 401(k)s and IRAs, Suze Orman is a great resource.

The basic difference between a traditional IRA and a Roth IRA is this… when you withdraw funds from a traditional IRA you have to pay taxes on your withdrawal [the same as you would with a 401(k)]. When funds are taken out of a Roth IRA, you don't pay taxes on your withdrawals. If you roll over your 401(k) into an IRA, the IRA will be a traditional IRA.

The incentive for getting a traditional IRA is that the amount you invest, you are able to write off on your taxes for that tax year. Your Roth IRA will be whatever your balance in your traditional IRA was minus taxes. When you do the conversion is important. Right now, as a young person, I assume you don't make much money and are therefore in the lowest tax bracket. As you get older, you'll make more money and be in a higher tax bracket. So, if you do the conversion now, you will pay less in taxes than if you do the conversion later on in life. If you do the conversion sooner rather than later your money can grow tax-free longer.

Start saving now. If you don't know which investments to put your money into, you can either do heavy research, or you can trust the company your retirement account is with and use one of their target date mutual funds. A mutual fund is a collection of stocks/ funds that is professionally managed and diversified. Most companies will continue to manage the fund even after you retire. Let the professionals make all of the investment decisions for you with a goal of maximizing your investment. Your money is pooled with everyone else in that fund which helps reduce how much you pay on administrative fees. Plus, your investments are professionally managed by those smarter than you and are routinely diversified. Generally, investments in target date mutual funds are riskier now, when you are younger, and gradually grow more conservative as time passes. Shifting gradually from more stocks now to more bonds later. The great thing about mutual funds, is that if one stock crashes out of thirty, the impact is minimal.

<u>Keep That Change</u>

Never throw change away. My friend John is notorious for just throwing all coin on the ground, literally. He just throws it away. Think about what would happen if you got a jug, and put all of your coins in that jug. When the jug is full, you will have hundreds of dollars saved up. We are poor enough as it is, so why throw money away?

<u>The Lucky Ones</u>

When living at home, you are lucky. I would love to live at home again because the stress of living alone at such a young age just plain sucks. While you are lucky enough to live at home, you should save your money. I am not telling you to not go out and have fun, but make sure you start putting money away and save. Want a tricked-out dorm room? It's gonna cost you money. Need coffee at 3 AM because you're pulling an all-nighter? It's gonna cost you money. Need to do anything, anywhere? It's gonna cost you money. The better you plan, the easier your life will be.

When you live at home, you don't pay for every bill. Utilities (such as gas, electric, cable, internet, water), rent, maintenance, repairs, and food are all, at least partially, paid for by your parents. When you live in your own apartment, all of that responsibility is yours.

Once you are off to college, you may be getting student loans. You may even be getting money from those loans for personal spending (books, lab fees, transportation, etc.), but eventually, you will have to pay that money back, with thousands of dollars in interest. As long as your schedule permits, you need to continue to work in college. By schedule, I mean your academic course load, not your social life. Life is full of sacrifices, so get a job, even if you don't have to. Save money and start making early payments to your loan. Trust me, paying a little now can shave years off of your loan repayment term. That means you will save hundreds, if not thousands, of dollars in interest in the future. So start making payments before you are required if you can, or make extra payments when you can. Just a little bit goes a long way.

The main factor, in my opinion, of reckless spending is a lack of respect for money. I am not saying that you need to let money run your life, but you must have respect for it. If you have respect for money and the limitations it imposes on you, then you will be set free from the shackles it has on your life. Respect it, plan how you use it, and you will see more of it. It may not be fun, but that's reality.

4
The Basics of Banking

No MATTER WHAT ANYONE SAYS OR DOES, YOU ARE THE ONE in charge of your finances. You are in control of your financial destiny. You can't blame anyone for the mistakes or mishaps that happen with your account. When push comes to shove, you are responsible for your account and your financial standing. You must take great care and responsibility if you wish to be treated like an adult in the world.

Making it Count

All right, let's cover the basics. In the business world (which includes the financial world), there are "Business Days" and "Non Business Days".
A business day is any regular day Monday through Friday (except for any federal holiday).

- A non-business day is Saturday, Sunday, and federal holidays that fall on Monday through Friday.

So, if you walk into a banking center on Sunday (yes, some banks are open 7 days a week) and you do a transaction, then you are processing a transaction on a non-business day. This means the transaction will be pending until it posts at the end of the next business day. All transactions done on Saturday, Sunday and Monday, count towards Monday's business day. So, if you have a credit card payment due on Saturday, you must make the payment by Friday or it will be considered late. A deposit done on Saturday morning posts at the same time as a deposit done Monday evening. Signs and notices are displayed informing you of when the bank will be closed for holidays and when their normal hours of operation are, so please plan accordingly. Currently, there is legislation mandating that banks have credit card/ loan due dates fall only on business days. To me, this is common sense.

One of the most confusing terms in banking is deciphering the difference between your "Current Balance" and your "Available Balance". These terms may vary from bank to bank, so check with your financial institution about the terms that they use. Generally, the following explanations apply.

Your *current* balance is your balance in your account at the beginning of that business day. This *does not* include anything that is pending on your account. For example, if your current balance Friday morning is $500, that is what your balance was after everything posted to your account Thursday night. If you get paid every Friday via direct deposit the $500 balance you begin the business day with does not include the $400 direct deposit you received that day. The reason your current balance doesn't reflect the direct deposit is because it officially has not posted to your account yet. If you get paid every Friday, the money will officially post to your account at the end of Friday's business day. The direct deposit is a part of your available balance and you are able to use the funds, but the transaction hasn't officially posted to your account.

An *available balance* is what is available for you to spend. Your available balance will include any money entering your account (a direct deposit, ATM deposit, or banking center deposit) and will include any money leaving your account (the purchase you just made getting gas, the student loan payment that is automatically taken out, and that withdrawal from the ATM). The available balance is the most accurate balance you have on your account and should be consulted before making any purchases. Many financial institutions have up to the second updates on your account. As soon as you swipe your bankcard, the bank will know it, therefore, you can check your available balance online, over the phone, at the ATM, or in a banking center immediately.

So remember, current= posted and available=able to use (includes pending transactions).

Where to Bank

Here are some key areas to look at when you are looking to open an account with a financial institution:

Does the bank have locations close to your job, school and home? It is crucial that your bank be near all three of these locations, if possible. You never know when you may need to run to the bank. Having the bank close by helps you foster a healthy relationship with that banking center and its associates and keeps you on track financially. The main reason this is good is because once those paychecks start rolling in, you will want to be close to the bank so you can immediately deposit your money, right? What's the point of making money if you can't spend it? Until you deposit your paycheck, it's useless; it has no actual monetary value.

Of course, you should enroll in direct deposit, if you can, and you won't have to worry about doing a deposit. If your job is in the service industry and you walk home with cash every night (such as being a server or bartender) you should still deposit your cash into your account as soon as possible, either through the ATM or at a teller the following day. If you keep cash in your wallet, it will be much more tempting to spend it. Furthermore, depositing your cash helps you save your money. What happens if you lose your wallet or you get mugged? I carry no more than $20 with me. If something were to happen to my wallet, I would only be out $20 or less. And with some ATMs now being able to count cash, you get immediate credit for cash deposited though them and not have to worry about your money being delayed going into your account.

Is the bank and it's accounts FDIC Insured? The FDIC stands for the Federal Deposit Insurance Corporation. Essentially, they are an insurance agency, which guarantees that you, the depositor, has access to your funds in the event that your bank should fail. As we have seen with the recession in late 2008 and early 2009, banks can fail. In those cases, anyone who had money in an account at one of the banks was still able to get their money, because the FDIC insured the banks and its deposits.

You, as a depositor, are protected up to $250,000 per financial institution. What does this mean to you? If you are lucky enough to have $250,000 in a bank account, you are protected. If the bank fails, the FDIC insures that you will get all of your money back. If you have more than that, I recommend opening up another account at a different bank, because, remember, it's $250,000 per financial institution. Of course, this is an overly simplistic explanation. Someone with this much money would have a private banker to help handle the complexities of financial protection and shielding.

The types of accounts that are FDIC Insured are: checking, savings, money market deposit accounts and CDs. Investment accounts are NOT FDIC insured because they invest in stocks, bonds, ETFs and mutual funds and those accounts are subject to the stock market and its fluctuations. Remember, there is no guarantee with the stock market.

For more information, check them out online at http://www.fdic.gov/

Are there Banking Centers all over the city/state/country or is it a local bank only with a few banking centers total? Some people who know they will stay in one area for the rest of their lives may opt to bank with a smaller bank for "better and more personal customer service." The down side to this scenario is when traveling; you won't have access to your financial institution. Larger financial institutions *should* provide the same quality of service as their smaller competitors but you have the added benefit of multiple banking centers in multiple areas. What works best for you? If you might be moving from the area that you currently live in (for college, perhaps) then it may be to your benefit to open an account and start building your financial relationship with a bank that provides national service. Longevity is key to a healthy financial relationship; so when you choose a bank, choose wisely, because you should plan to use them for a long time.

Does the bank have a large ATM network or do you have to use other banks' ATMs? Being close to ATMs is important because you never know when you may need cash or when you will need to do a deposit. If your bank has a large ATM network, you won't have to worry about going out of network to access your cash and be charged a fee. If your bank's ATMs are few and far between, it may prove stressful and aggravating to accomplish your banking needs. More on out of network ATM fees a little later on in this chapter.

Is the financial institution you bank with in the city/state where you are planning on attending college? Just so you know, banking laws and regulations vary from state to state. Make sure once you move, you introduce yourself to your local banking center and find out if there are any major changes in policy that differ from where you were to where you are. Examples of policy changes could be: fund availability and how easily they can service your account. So plan ahead! Now, you shouldn't have to open a new account when you move to a different state, that's the great thing about banking with a big bank, you can do interstate deposits. Don't let a bank talk you into opening a new account just because you moved so they can meet their new accounts opened goal. The point of banking with a large financial institution is that you don't have to do that. Obviously, extraneous circumstances come up and you may have to, but most of the time you don't. Remember, longevity with an account is key.

Home is Where the Heart is

In banking, the state you opened your account in almost always makes a difference in how your transaction is processed. Now, to me, this makes common sense. If your account was opened in Arizona, it will ALWAYS be an Arizona account. If you move to New York and change your address with the bank, you will still have an Arizona account because Arizona is where the account was originally opened. Changing your address doesn't change the past. This is important to know because in order to process your transaction for you, the teller needs to know where the account was originally opened, especially if it's different than the state you are currently in.

When I worked for Bank of America in New York City, the following was a common situation. A teller would ask a customer "Which state did you open your account in?" The customer would respond by saying their account is a New York account. When the transaction was processed the state was wrong. Again, the teller would ask what state the account was opened in and the customer undeniably responded with something along the lines of "I changed my account to a New York account when I changed my address". No. Wrong. Try again.

If this happens, you may be asked to fill out another deposit slip. You are now wasting not only the teller's time, but everyone else's who is waiting in line as well. Be prepared when you go into the banking center. Have your deposit slip filled out before you step up to the teller, and of course, make sure you fill out the right slip.

All of this hassle of filling out the wrong form then refilling out the new form could, of course, be avoided if you used your pre-printed deposit slips from the bank or did your deposit through the ATM.

The Long Haul

In banking, longevity is crucial to a healthy financial relationship. So, it's best to not keep switching banks, or closing and reopening an account. It is in your best interest to find the bank that works best for you, and stay with them.

Longevity, or how long you have been with the bank, works in your benefit when asking for favors or applying for lines of credit.

Favors that could be asked for are:
- Cashing a large check
- Waiving the fee for a cashiers check,
- Overriding a hold or delay of funds

Benefits in the realm of lines of credit can be:
- Low APRs
- No balance transfer fees
- A premium card with no annual fee

If you consistently close and reopen an account, you lose any longevity you had. So, do your homework beforehand and make an informed decision. It's just like moving around. If, as a kid, you move from school to school, you have to learn a new campus (banking center), make new friends (tellers), and learn all about the school rules (banking policy). For the most part it's similar, but with very nuanced differences.

Actions Speak Louder than Words

From the moment that your account is open, you begin building a relationship with that financial institution. Don't give the bank a reason to put a bad mark against your account in their systems. If you are in need of a favor (possibly cashing a large check not drawn off that particular financial institution), a customer with a perfect track record (a positive average balance and not being in the negative, possibly multiple accounts in good standing) will get the check cashed more so than a customer who has a shoddy relationship with the bank (someone who is constantly in the negative).

You should make an excellent first impression with the bank and have that impression last. It is in your best interest to keep your standing with the bank in the best possible shape and look as good as you can from the bank's point of view. Furthermore, being in good standing with your financial institution gives you the opportunity to receive special promotional deals. If you are a risky customer, don't count on receiving any special help.

You can keep your account in good shape by having:
- Direct Deposit
- A healthy (and positive) average balance
- Longevity
- No overdrafts
- Other accounts with the financial institution- Credit card, savings, CD, IRA

Special Promotional deals that banks offer are:
- Credit cards with a low APR
- A payment holiday (not having to pay a month) on your loan account
- Low or $0 fee balance transfers to low APR lines of credit (to consolidate debt)

<u>Working Hard for the Money</u>

When you get a job, the first thing you should do is enroll in direct deposit, if it's available. Direct deposit, as mentioned before, is where your employer electronically deposits your paycheck into your account on payday. You should enroll because it's the easiest way to be paid. To enroll, your employer should give you a form to fill out, or you can simply give them a voided check (they need this in order to get your routing and account numbers). A voided check is a check with the word "VOID" written across it.

There are many benefits to receiving your pay with direct deposit.
• Immediate availability of funds
• No delay of funds when depositing your paycheck (no holds)
• No waiting for the post office or inner-office mail to deliver your check
• Your check can't get lost in the mail
• Qualify for a free account with your financial institution
• No trips to the bank to deposit the check
• No forgetting to go to the bank
• No forgetting the check at home
• If out of town on vacation or not at work the day checks are distributed, you still receive your pay on time.
• Ease of mind knowing that the money will be there and you don't have to worry about it
• No overdraft fees because you thought you had enough money in your account and didn't because your check hadn't cleared.
• Split your pay to go into different accounts (for example: 75% of pay into your checking and 25% into your savings. Or $50 into savings and the remainder into your checking account. Two simple and quick ways to save money)
• It's easier to save because it's done automatically

You shouldn't be afraid of direct deposit. It is safer than carrying around an actual live check and you receive your funds faster. You'll still receive a pay stub, which will show you hours worked, taxes taken out, and other pertinent information regarding your employment. Not all employers offer direct deposit so if your work does, you must utilize this financial tool.

Direct Deposit is the most convenient way for both you and your employer to distribute your pay. Direct deposit is the easiest thing you can do to set yourself up on the path to financial independence and maturity.

Fees! Fees! Fees!

Fees are becoming outrageous in the world of banking and banks make money off of fees they charge their customers. Don't give them your money in fees because of poor managerial skills on your behalf. If you manage your account wisely, you can bank for free.

Do you pay a fee to use the ATM? For most, if not all, banks withdrawing cash from an ATM that they own is fee free. If you go "out-of-network" your financial institution may charge you a fee along with the financial institution who owned that ATM. Going out-of-network means you used a different financial institution's ATM to take care of your financial needs. Why waste $4 in fees just to take out $20? That's a 20% fee! Stick with your bank and your network and save yourself the fee. Your bank shouldn't charge you to take money out of one of their ATMs, if they do, change banks immediately.

Banks justify this very common fee in the banking world as a courtesy fee because you are essentially taking money away from their customers to take care of your needs. And the needs of a non-customer aren't the primary focus of the bank.

The closest comparison I can think of is that an ATM out of network fee is like roaming on a cell phone. You are charged extra when you use your cell phone out of your network and use another carrier's networks. It's the same scenario here.

Some banks (generally smaller institutions) offer no fee, a reduced fee, or fee reversal for their customers on the fees imposed for out-of-network ATM use as an incentive to bank with them. Larger banks have an extensive ATM network, so it should be easy to locate one of their ATMs. Which method of banking works best for you? Decide, and then open an account with that bank. It's a good idea to do your research and remember these key facts when choosing your bank. How do banks stack up against one another in your mind?

Currently, Bank of America offers the largest ATM network across the country with over 18,000 ATMs. Chase offers the largest ATM network in New York City.

A tip on how to avoid an out of network ATM fee is to go to a grocery store and buy something (a candy bar) and get cash back. You are still getting the cash you need, but with no fees from any financial institution. Not all stores do this, and more stores do this outside of major metropolitan areas, so do some research. Once you know the rules of the game, you can easily win. Just a side note here, you can only get cash back on debit card transactions, not credit.

Personal Bankers ARE NOT Miracle Workers

Personal bankers are the people you speak to when you need to service your account. Servicing an account could mean changing your contact information, opening a new account or making a withdrawal from your CD. It is ideal to have a good rapport with a personal banker because this allows them to give you specialized service when you come in.

If you get into a financial situation and you need help or guidance, go to your banking center and speak to a personal banker or supervisor. Tell them your situation and get the help you need. They can help you form habits to prevent future fees. I warn you though, don't be greedy. If a fee is reversed for you, do not constantly ask for every fee you incur to be reversed. You should figure out why you are being assessed fees and work to rectify your habits.

Every time a fee is reversed, that is a loss of profit on the bank's behalf. Reversal of fees is getting so strict, some banks require a personal banker to explain why they reversed the fees they did. If the personal banker does too many favors for you or for others they may lose their job, leaving you without a person to go to for help. Something else that could happen is the personal banker could just stop helping you with fees in general.

5
Deposits

Putting Money in the Bank

In an effort to make depositing money easier for customers, many banks offer free pre-printed deposit slips, or a book of deposit slips for a small fee. It is to your benefit to get these and to use them. Pre-printed deposit slips are for your convenience and ease, and to help process your transaction more quickly and efficiently. They also prevent you from writing down the account number incorrectly. A pre-printed deposit slip is the same size as a standard check. Your name and address are printed in the upper left hand corner and your routing number and account number, at the bottom.

There are many benefits to using a pre-printed deposit slip.
1. You don't have to write all of your personal information every time you go into a bank to do a deposit. If you use a generic/ blank deposit slip provided to you in the lobby of the banking center **_YOU_** must fill out your information! The teller cannot fill it out for you

2. The teller can scan the deposit slip and the computer will immediately know the state your account was opened in and the account number. This eliminates the slight chance that your transaction will be processed incorrectly. (For example, your money being deposited into the wrong account).

3. Errors are reduced because there is no possibility of the teller misreading sloppy handwriting and depositing your money into someone else's account

4. Prevents having the transaction reversed all together by a Transaction Proof Operator who cannot read your handwriting.

5. If an error does occur, then your contact information and account number will already be legibly provided to those trying to rectify your situation. This is a great reason to always have accurate contact information with the bank.

6. You don't accidentally fill out the wrong form for your deposit, which would result in rewriting a brand new deposit slip or being asked to get to the back of the line.

The bottom line is: your deposit will be completed more quickly and accurately.

If you *must* fill out a generic deposit slip, make sure you grab the proper form and fill out ALL of your information neatly. There wouldn't be a line for the information if it weren't required. The teller isn't your mother; you are an adult, so fill out your own deposit slip. And when you do fill out your own deposit slip, don't make the teller and then subsequently the proof operator, struggle to read your handwriting. Neat handwriting or a pre-printed deposit slip benefits everyone.

When filling out a deposit slip, if you don't know your account number by heart (through self memorization) then bring it on a piece of paper or have it programmed in your cell phone. I would recommend the latter because paper is easily lost and everyone is glued to his or her cell phone. Even if you don't know your account number, you can still fill out the rest of the deposit slip and have the teller look up the number for you, via your debit card.

One of my biggest pet peeves is when people don't fill out a deposit slip at all. I hated that. Not knowing your account number doesn't mean you don't know your name and how much you are depositing!

Tellers can use your bankcard (ATM card, Check/ Debit Card) to search for your account number. In order to do this, you may have to show ID, so make sure it's government issued and non-expired.

Filling out a Deposit Slip

I will now go over the easy steps on how to do a deposit.

1. Fill out the date on your pre-printed deposit slip or fill out the *entire* slip for a generic deposit slip

2. List the cash you are depositing in the cash row and the checks you are depositing in the checks row. If you don't have one of these items (just depositing cash or just depositing checks), then leave that row blank. If you are depositing more checks than there are check rows, then you can use one row for the subtotal of all of the checks. To get the subtotal, turn your pre-printed deposit slip over and you will see more rows for checks. Note, if you are depositing cash, you may not be able to do a deposit requiring cash back in the same transaction. The easiest thing would be to get change from the teller before the deposit, then perform the straight deposit with the correct totals.

3. If you are depositing checks and receiving cash back (doing a less cash deposit) make sure you sign the appropriate line approving the cash back.

4. Make sure that your deposit slip is filled out *before* you reach the teller. This saves everyone time. The slip should be completely filled out with all of your information. There wouldn't be a line for that

information if it wasn't needed. Make sure everything is added up and complete and that you know how much you are depositing before you reach the teller. I have seen it happen where the customer just trusts the teller to count their cash and trust the number they come up with. While tellers are mostly accurate, we are all human, and what if the teller accidentally miscounts and shorts you $100 in your deposit?

5. Present the deposit to the teller.
6. Check your receipt for accuracy at the end of your transaction (account number, transaction amount, etc.).

When depositing a check you either receive the funds immediately or the next business day as long as no holds are placed. Immediate credit of checks is only possible in certain states with certain financial institutions. You should be aware of fund availability so you can plan accordingly when making your deposits. For the majority of America, when depositing a check you will receive a small portion immediately (generally $100) and then get the remainder of the funds the next business day (as long as there is no hold placed on the check). This delay allows for the bank to begin processing the check in an effort to reduce and prevent fraud.

Of course, you could always use an ATM for your deposit, which is quick, easy and reliable. Some banks, Bank of America and Chase for example, don't even require a deposit slip or an envelope for an ATM deposit. Their ATMs count cash and scan checks immediately and process transactions in a similar fashion to the way tellers do. Cash goes in immediately and checks should get some funds immediately with the remaining funds the following business day.

Doing an ATM deposit is easy. Though the process may be slightly skewed from bank to bank, these are generic instructions for how to do an ATM deposit.

ATM Deposit with an Envelope:

1. Count the cash and/or checks beforehand and know your total deposit amount.
2. Place the deposit material inside of an ATM deposit envelope.
3. Dip your card into the ATM and key in your pin number
4. Choose the option "Deposit"
5. Key in the total amount of your deposit
6. Choose the account the money is entering
7. Place the envelope into the machine (look for prompts so you place the envelope in machine the correct way)
8. Grab your receipt and verify the information on the slip

ATM Deposit where the machine counts cash and scans checks:

1. Count the cash and/or checks beforehand and know your total deposit amount.
2. Dip your card into the ATM and key in your pin number
3. Choose the option "Deposit"
4. Choose the account the money is entering
5. Choose either "Cash" or "Checks"
6. Place the cash or checks into machine separately. If doing a deposit with both, deposit one group first, then once that has been counted click the option to either "Add Cash" or "Add Checks"
7. Finish the deposit
8. Grab your receipt and verify the information on the slip

When you do an ATM deposit in an envelope you receive a portion of the funds immediately and the remainder the following business day. This means that ATM deposits, in most parts of the country are just as fast as doing your deposit with the teller. You can deposit cash and checks because the machine doesn't know what is in the envelope. The only down side to an envelope ATM deposit is you don't get cash immediately, because as I just mentioned, the machine doesn't know what is in the envelope.

Mistakes Happen

An error can occur with any transaction because humans and technology aren't perfect. Even a simple deposit can be processed incorrectly. The most common errors/ mistakes are: misreading an account number and depositing into an account in the wrong state.

If an account number is written out on a generic deposit slip and the teller or Proof Operator (the people who review every transaction for accuracy) misreads your handwriting, your transaction may get reversed. If a deposit is reversed, then the money will be taken out of your account, leaving you without those funds. Fees could be incurred if you were relying on that money to go towards a purchase you made. Furthermore, if you don't fill out your generic deposit slip with all of the required information legibly, then how is the bank supposed to contact you? It's important to keep your receipts because if an error occurs, the receipt has information the bank can use to resolve your problem. It's also proof your deposit occurred.

Some banks have different deposit slips for accounts opened in different states (i.e. one form for accounts opened in the state you are actually in and a form for all accounts outside of that state). This is called doing an in-state deposit and an out-of-state deposit. A pre-printed deposit slip would eliminate the possible error of you filling out the wrong deposit slip. Just a note, some financial institutions have one slip for all accounts and the state the account was opened in doesn't matter. Check with your bank about what their process is.

If, for example, you have a California account and travel to Rhode Island and make a deposit using a Rhode Island deposit slip, the deposit might not go through. There are two possible reasons for this:

1. You fill out the generic form completely with your name and address and you put your account number on the form like you are supposed to. Though you made your deposit with the correct account number, the account number and the state don't match up. Causing you to fill out a brand new form.

2. You fill out the generic form completely with your name and address and you put your account number on the form like you are supposed to. If fate is working against you, you might have the same account number as someone else who resides in another state. So, it's possible your money will be placed into another person's account, thus causing your deposit to not be processed into your account.

I have an example of the second scenario. A close friend of mine went into a bank and deposited $300 in cash into his checking account. He filled out a generic deposit slip and presented it to the teller. His account was opened in that state and when the transaction was complete he kept his receipt and went about his business. When he checked online, the money was not in his account. He checked again the next day and it was the same story, his money was not there. This should have been the first red flag, because cash is always available right away. After returning to that original banking center and speaking to a personal banker, the destination of his funds was discovered.

My friend filled out his account number incorrectly because he didn't know his account number by heart. He started putting in his debit card number then stopped when he ran out of space. The numbers on my friend's check card happened to be the account number of someone else. So what happened was, the teller didn't verify the name on the account and the money went into an account in a different state.

Here were the mistakes the bank made:

1. The names on the account didn't match. The teller should have noticed this and confirmed which account was the correct one

2. The account was in a different state, the teller should have noticed this and confirmed which state was the correct one

3. Since debit cards and account numbers are pretty formulaic per state and per bank, the teller should have verified the account number and the name on the account.

Here were the mistakes my friend made:

1. He should have been prepared with a pre-printed deposit slip

2. He should have known his account number

3. Since he didn't know his account number, he should've asked the teller to look it up

4. He could have just done an ATM deposit and avoided the hassle

This is what went right, after the fact:

1. My friend kept his receipt. Every receipt has important information the bank needs in order to investigate a discrepancy

2. My friend returned to the original banking center where the transaction happened

You cannot rely on the teller to do the double-checking for you. Why trust someone else with something that is important to you? Why not double-check yourself, just to be sure? The more prepared you are, the better equipped you are in this world. Hopefully you can learn from my friend's situation and not have this happen to you.

Something is Wrong! What do I do?

If a transaction is processed and there is an error, contact the financial institution as soon as possible.

Always keep your teller receipts; they are your proof of each transaction. If there is an error, you can prove you made your deposit. Also, a receipt is your way of checking, in the exact moment of the transaction, to verify everything is correct (amount of transaction and account number).

Don't hate the player, hate the game

When you go into a banking center, a teller's job is to tell you about the products and services the bank offers that can help you achieve your financial goals. When you call customer service over the phone, they have the same job as a teller, to inform you of products and services the bank offers. And finally, when you sign into Online Banking, there will be ads and even separate pages that you are automatically routed to which informs you of a special deal or promotion that the bank is offering you. I will be the first to admit that I hate being sold things I don't need, but you never know, the offer could be a special service you could truly benefit from. So keep an open mind and don't get upset at the teller for doing their jobs.

If you are offered a special promotion (inside a banking center, on the phone, or online) listen to / read the information closely. The offer may only be offered at that time and not offered in the future. Furthermore, if you are offered a deal online, it may not be available inside a banking center. My point is, seize the opportunity if it is something that could help you! Never say no before you know what the offer is.

A few examples of special promotions are:
1) Receiving a $50 credit to open a checking account online, but that same offer is not available if you go into the banking center.

2) If you apply for a credit card online you will receive 0% APR for one full year, but inside the banking center that special (and great) deal isn't offered.

3) If you are inside the banking center and a teller tells you that you were pre-approved, based on your relationship, for a credit card with 0% interest on purchases and balance transfers for six months. If you say no you may not be offered the deal again.

4) If you open your checking or savings account online, it will be free for life. No direct deposit minimums and no balance requirements.

5) Performing a balance transfer from multiple cards onto one card with a low interest rate for debt consolidation.

These are all great deals! If you turn it down, you may not be offered the deal again. Going back after the fact (going back into the banking center, signing back into Online Banking or calling customer service) may not help you regain that offer.

Don't be irritated because you are being offered something. Simply listen to what is being offered to you, it may be the perfect opportunity to consolidate your debt or receive a bonus for banking with that particular bank. Listen and decide if that promotion is right for you.

Never, EVER, be rude to a teller. I say this because it is personal to me. It's just common human decency to be nice to people. How would you like it if someone came to your job and yelled at you?

Prove It!

Some banks offer a service that allows you to do basic transactions without showing ID. Sound too good to be true? It isn't! The process works like this: you swipe your debit card through a machine that is linked to the teller's computer; you enter in your pin number, and presto, you're done. The theory is, only the true owner of the account will be in possession of the card and know the PIN. So, when you verify that information, it is sufficient ID to do most basic transactions. If your banking center offers this service, trust them and have the bank work for you and utilize the services they offer. The bank is not trying to steal your identity with the machines. The way I know that is, the bank already has all of your information, if they wanted to steal your identity, they would have already.

Your social security number can be used to search for your account number and account information, but this should be your last resort. If you have to use your social security number, you must provide the teller with a valid, non-expired government ID to verify your identity. For your safety, write down your social security number for the teller on a piece of paper and give it to them. When the teller is finished with the number, have the *teller* dispose of the number for you. Banks go through great efforts to protect your information. I would trust throwing away important information at a bank over throwing it away at home, even if you own a shredder.

Some assume that a teller can search for their account information by using their name. This however, is one of the worst ways to search for account information. It is shocking how many people share a name, especially those with common names. Can you even imagine how many Maria Hernandez's there are in the world?

Equality for All

One of the most aggravating things in banking is a customer who thinks they are above waiting in line. Everyone waits in line. I know how frustrating it is to see two tellers working when there are ten people in line. I really do. That still gives me no right to cut everyone in line and demand to be helped by a teller. Cutting in line only makes the other customers angry as well as the tellers and causes everyone to wait longer, including you. It doesn't matter if you have $1 vested in that bank or $1 million; you are a person just like everyone else. Wait your turn!

<u>Welcome to the Internet</u>

With online banking you have control over your account whenever you want. Online banking is a platform on the Internet that allows you to complete basic transactions and service requests on any of your accounts with that particular financial institution. You sign in using a username and password and then you are automatically linked to all of your accounts. Once inside you can transfer funds between accounts, make payments to loans and credit cards, set up automatic bill pay, change your address and phone number, request a credit line increase on your credit card, and so much more.

Bill pay is the ability to pay for bills that you have with vendors (utilities, cell phone, cable, etc) directly from your account. You fill in the information of where the bill is going and for how much and when you want it paid, and your bank takes care of the rest. They write a check for you and send it to your vendor, which saves you on postage. Bill pay is just one of the many services you get for free with online banking.

Online banking is a per financial institution thing, meaning that you can only see your accounts with online banking per financial institution. If you have accounts at different banks, you won't be able to see them in the same online banking interface. You would have to sign into each individual banks' online banking since they are separate companies.

<u>Safety First</u>

Banks go through strenuous measures to protect your information and your identity. With that said, only the person or persons on an account can receive information about said account (balance, a transaction posting or pending, etc.). This includes searching for an account number.

If your parents live in Utah and you move to Vermont for college, unless your mom and/or dad are on your account they CANNOT view information on your account. It is a violation of federal law which protects your financial information. Make sure your parents understand this as well. Many parents go into a banking center and try and do a deposit for their child but don't have the account number. The teller legally cannot search for your account number because the bank would then be verifying that you have an account with that financial institution.

Furthermore, parents cannot ask for a balance or any information on the account. Parents will argue that they are your parent and they need to know. That's great, but they still aren't getting information on the account. If you want your parents to have access to this information, add them to your account. It's just the same as if someone were asking for information on a strangers account. How does the teller know that a particular person truly is your parent? What if the account owner is estranged from their parents? Banks don't want to get involved in personal affairs, so only account owners can get account information. This is for your protection.

People not on an account can still do a cash deposit into an account they are not on. So, if your parents want to deposit money in your account there are many ways of doing so.

• You can give your parents your account number, and your parents can come in and fill out a blank deposit slip (completely of course, including your account number) and then do the deposit.

• You could order deposit slips (which are generally free) and give your parents a booklet.

• You and your parents can set up an online transfer. When transferring money between two accounts online where you aren't an owner on both, the transfer is a one-way street. If your parents add your account as a "payee" account, they are able to transfer money from their account to your account, that's it. Your parents will not have access to any information on your account (balance, etc.) and they will not have power to take money from your account. Furthermore, you will not have access to transfer funds from their account; only your parents can do that. Online transfers should be free if it's within the same financial institution, if transferring from one bank to another, there could be a fee.

A teller can't search for an account number for a non-owner, even if they are a parent or family member and even if the teller doesn't give this person the account number. Many parents try to break the law by telling the teller to just deposit the money and not tell them the account number. A teller legally can't do that, since the account owner didn't authorize the search for their account number. If the teller finds your account number (even if the person provides ALL information about your account except for the account number) the teller would be verifying to the non-owner that the person they are inquiring about has an account with that bank. What if you didn't want a person to know where you banked?

Here is an example. Let's say that a man and woman are married. Since they are married they share an account and have access to one another's information. Now, let's say the man is abusive and beats his wife. She finally escapes from him, moves to a different state, and starts her life over. If the ex-husband walks into different financial institutions and says "My wife wants me to do a deposit for her, but I don't have the account number, but here is her social security number, can you do the deposit?" The answer is no. If the teller does the deposit, then that teller just told the ex-husband where his ex-wife banks, placing him one-step closer to finding her. This may be an extreme example, but I've seen this happen.

I know that my parents bank with Bank of America. This is common knowledge in my family and I worked for Bank of America for two and a half years; it's just something I know. Now, just because I personally know Bank of America is where they bank, I cannot go into a banking center and have the teller search for their account number. If a teller did search and find my parents' account number, they would be verifying for me that my parents bank with Bank of America, which is a breach of security of my parents' behalf. All of these precautions are for your safety!

If you want someone to do a deposit into your account, *you* must provide him or her with your account number. You can locate your account number by going into a banking center and showing valid ID, through online banking, calling customer service, or looking at the bottom of one of your personal checks or deposit slips.

You can avoid possible stress by having both you and your parents go into a banking center and you can add your parents as co-owners to your account. If you do this, they will have complete access to everything on your account. They have the ability to take money out of the account, track what you are spending your money on, and monitor your habits. Find what's best for you and your parents, then make the appropriate steps to achieving your financial goals!

6
Checking

I KNOW THE WORLD OF ADULT BANKING CAN BE SCARY, with minimum balances, direct deposit, multiple accounts, payment due dates, etc. So...take a deep breath and let's take this on, step by step.

Your First Account

The following are some key points you should consider before you open your first account:

Do you get an account where your parent's bank or do you go elsewhere?
Many young adults bank where their parents bank. This can be good or bad, depending on how you look at the situation.

Possible Pros:
- Advantage of already banking somewhere where a relationship has already been established
- Possible free account
- Ease of the family banking in one place (easy online transfers and carpooling to the bank).
- Parents can help teach you how to bank based on their experiences with that financial institution.

Possible Cons:
- There might be a better banking offer for you, personally, elsewhere
- You don't get the independence you are looking for because your parents are guiding your every move
- Your parent's local bank may not fit into your plans once you move away from home

My accounts are with the same bank as my family, so it's all a matter of preference.

This is what my financial picture looks like:
- One checking account with my parents as co-owners.
- Two savings accounts (One with my parents at a traditional bank and one by myself through an online bank)
- Three credit cards (One for everyday purchases, one for overdraft protection, and one for business expenses)

Do you get an account with your parent's as a co-owner or do you want the freedom and independence of your own account?

If your parents are on your account they have just as much power as you do with the account. This means, they are able to withdraw cash, get a statement of purchases and deposit money at will. If you, or your parents, overdraw the account, both you are your parents are responsible for the negative balance. If the balance isn't taken care of, both parties will have to deal with the negative repercussions. Having your own account gives you privacy, knowing that only you know what you are doing with your account. Keep in mind if you get your own account, you are on your own. All the responsibility is yours.

There is a misconception, especially with parents, that a person has to be on an account to deposit cash into it. This is why many parents want to be a co-owner of your checking account. This is untrue. Anyone with your account number can deposit cash into your account. Your parents can still deposit cash/ transfer money into your account, all you need to do is give them your account number.

Most banks offer premium service to their more prominent or business customers, if your parents fall into this category, having one or both of them on your account should give you the same premium service. So, what's more important, privacy or premium products?

Possible financial perks of being an Advantage/Premier/Select Customer:
- Interest Checking Accounts (a checking account that accrues interest)
- Higher interest rates on savings accounts and lower rates on lines of credit.
- Built-in longevity and credibility
- Free accounts
- Less chance of a hold being placed on a check (delay of funds)
- Free bank checks (Money Orders, Cashiers Checks and personal checks)

Does the bank offer a free checking account?
Most banks offer free checking accounts for students. If you don't get a free account and you are a student, look around. I recommended getting a student account either by yourself, so you could start becoming independent and be in charge of your own finances, or with a parent. If you aren't a student, you

can get a free account with most banks if you have a regular direct deposit, such as a paycheck. If you want to be treated and respected as an adult, you have to act like one. Some banks offer you a limited amount of fee reversals for student accounts. They understand that things might come up, and you are still learning how to manage your money. This fee reversal is the bank's way of offering you one chance to mess up, and not have to pay for it. So, learn your monetary lessons quickly. One last note, if you are a minor, you must have a parent as a co-signer on your account.

If you want a completely free account but aren't a student, do some research and find a deal out there for you. Most banks offer a free account if you have direct deposit or a credit card with them. Some banks will offer you a completely free account as long as you open it online, instead of inside of a banking center. Having a free account, however, does not prevent you from being charged fees you may cause, such as an overdraft fee.

ChexSystems

The student checking account is supposed to ease you into becoming in control of your finances. You must remember a student checking account is still a real account. This means that you are still liable for any overdrafts you incur, and if the account closes in the negative, you will be submitted to ChexSystems. According to ChexSystems' website "ChexSystems, Inc network is comprised of member Financial Institutions that regularly contribute information on mishandled checking and savings accounts to a central location. ChexSystems shares this information among member institutions to help them assess the risk of opening new accounts." Essentially, it's a database of people who owe money to a financial institution. Once in ChexSystems you will be on file for years unless the institution that submitted you requests you be removed. Being in ChexSystems can prevent you from getting a checking or savings account, credit card, loan, or mortgage with a financial institution. So, if you think that not taking care of your overdraft is okay, think twice. You can learn more about ChexSystems at their website which can be found at https://www.consumerdebit.com/

Debit Cards

When you open a checking account, you have the option to get a debit card (also known as your check card). The debit card will have either a Visa or MasterCard logo. It is with your debit card that you can go to any merchant, swipe your card, and make a purchase. The funds for that purchase are taken directly from the checking account you have linked to that card, and, more often than not, funds are taken out that same day.

ATM cards *do not* have a Visa or MasterCard logo on it. The lack of logo does not allow you to make purchases at merchants like your debit card does. Both ATM and debit cards have a PIN and can be used at an ATM to withdraw cash and do deposits; however, the ATM card can only be used at the ATM.

Just because your debit card has a Visa or MasterCard logo on it doesn't mean it is an actual credit card. You can use the card as credit, but that doesn't make it a credit card. A credit card is a card that has a credit limit that you use then pay back. A debit card pulls funds directly from your checking account with funds you already have. A credit card purchase is loaned money and will have to be paid back.

If you use your debit card and have the company process the transaction as credit, you cannot get cash back like you can with a debit purchase. Cash back is where the merchant charges you more than what your actual total is and gives you the difference. For example, you go to a grocery store and your total is $50. If you want $20 cash back, then the total amount charged would be $70, and the cashier will hand you a $20 bill. Many places generally give cash back in increments of $10 or $20 for no fee. Cash back is a luxury, not a requirement, so some places may not offer cash back. Cash back is beneficial if you aren't near an ATM in your network.

The biggest difference in using a debit card for either credit or debit is when the funds will be taken out of your checking account. If you use your debit card and process the transaction as debit, then the funds *should* leave your account that night. If you use your debit card and process the transaction as credit, then the funds will leave your account in two to three business days. Generally.

Banks used to put a person's account number on their bankcard, but banks are slowly moving away from this. If a person loses their bankcard, a new one can just be ordered with a new number. However, if a bankcard with someone's account number is lost, it puts that person more at risk of fraudulent activity on his or her account. So giving your bankcard number to a friend or parent as your account number will not work. Yes, the teller can use that number to find your account number, but only for you. A teller can't use your bankcard number to find your account number for your friends or your mom.

If your bankcard is lost or stolen, just call customer service or go into a banking center and re-order a new one. It's that simple. You do NOT need to close your account and reopen a new one. When you do that, you start a brand new relationship with the bank with that account. You should only close and reopen your account if your account number has been compromised.

Posting

Posting means when funds actually leave your account. Posting is *NOT* the bank's responsibility. If the merchant doesn't close out your transaction at the end of the night, then the funds they have on hold for the purchase must legally be released back into your account. The funds, however, will come out whenever the merchant does close the transaction, which may be several days later. Trust me, the merchant will not forget to charge you. It's not the bank's fault if the grocery store takes four business days to close your transaction and take your money out at the end of those four days. This is why having a handwritten checkbook register is vital, as well as overdraft protection. Be aware of your balances.

Credits post to an account before debits do. Meaning money going in will post before money comes out. Now, there is a rumor that larger debits will post first on an account because it increases the likelihood that you may overdraw, thus creating revenue for the bank. I don't know if this is true or not, but if it is, get overdraft protection and don't worry about it!

A merchant can only hold your funds for one business day. At the end of that business day, the merchant must either close out your transaction and take your funds, or relinquish the money back into your account. If the latter situation occurs, the merchant still has a right to your money. When the transaction officially posts, it may not show as pending on your account beforehand. This is *NOT* a bank error. Even more so, it's *NOT* the bank's fault you didn't keep track of your money and your account went into the negative.

What does it mean to you if the funds are taken out four days later? This has gotten many of my friends into financial trouble. If you have $100 in your account and you make your cell phone payment of $75, you are left with $25. Now, let's say two days later the cell phone company hasn't deducted the funds from your account yet and you check your balance and your balance is still $100. You think you have more money than what you really do and decide to go shopping. You go to the mall and buy lunch and a few shirts from a store. Overall, for the day, you spend $40. But that's fine, because your balance showed that you had $100 in your account, right? The next day you check your balance, and it's in the negative by $53. How did this happen? I will explain....

Your cell phone payment was taken out that night, even though you had "paid" two days earlier. Since they already had authorization for the funds but couldn't legally hold them for longer than 24 hours the funds were released back into your account. The cell phone company closed out your transaction last night and collected the funds guaranteed to them, leaving your remaining balance at $25. Your shirts at the store cost you $30, bringing your account into the negative by $5. After a $10 lunch, your account now sits at negative $15. Once the transactions post that night, you have two transactions, which brought your account into the negative. You were then assessed two low overdraft fees at $19 each, one for the clothing purchase and another for lunch. The transactions were processed because your current balance had sufficient funds when the card was swiped.

This could've been avoided if you just kept a manual checkbook of your purchases.

Recent financial reform legislation is trying to prevent your account from overdrawing by processing authorizations for purchases to be based on your available balance instead of your current balance. While it is a step forward, the responsibility still lies with you to be aware of your own finances. Keep in mind; if you have an automatic payment that comes up without pending first, your account can still be overdrawn. The law makes the exception for automatic payments and checks because the assumption is those items are probably important and you'd rather have them paid than declined. You can opt out of this if you wish.

If you use your debit card and process the transaction as credit, the funds will be placed on hold for that business day then released back into your account until the funds are deducted from your account permanently. Credit transactions take longer to post than debit transactions, generally about two or three business days. If the transaction stays pending for multiple days, it's probably getting reauthorized each day.

Many customers are infuriated that their debit and credit card still works even if there is no money in their account or credit available. While each individual instance is unique and there are multiple factors in explaining why this happens, one possible explanation is that authorizations are based on current, not available, balances. That means that as long as your current balance is positive, then the authorization can still be given. So, if you started off the business day with enough money to cover the charge, the merchant you are at gets authorization based off of your balance at the beginning of the day, not the balance at that exact moment. The same principle applies to credit cards.

Regulation E

There has been recent legislation passed to prevent credit and debit authorizations from being processed if it will cause you to overdraw or go over your credit limit. While the regulation I am about to explain applies only to depository accounts (your checking) the same principal will apply to lines of credit (credit cards).

Regulation E states that any POS (point of sale) transactions will be declined at the merchant if you don't have the funds to cover the purchase unless you opt in to allow overdrafts on your account. So, if you go to Starbucks and use your card, if you don't have the funds in your account, the bank will decline the transaction, unless you have already specified with the bank that you would rather not have any of your purchases declined.

There are three categories within Reg E. I like to call it "All, some or none." You can either have all transactions go through and incur an overdraft, only some of your transactions go through (such as a recurring payments and checks) and incur an overdraft on only those with all other transactions declined, or you can have NONE of the transactions get paid.

Reg E's default is to put everyone in the "some" category, as it assumes you would want your recurring payments (student loans, insurance, car payments) and checks to go through, but are okay with being declined on other purchases.

If you choose the "None" category, then recurring payments will be declined and may cause you a fee from the person who was denied their payment. If your rent check gets returned on your landlord that may require you to pay rent in the future with bank checks, which could become costly and would require you to go into a bank.

I can't tell you which category is best for you, but the "some" category is what I would recommend.

The Internet

When using the Internet in order to purchase any good or service, you, as a consumer, are more protected when you use your credit card than your debit card, generally. The most important reason is this: when making a purchase with your debit card, it relies on you, the consumer, to prove that you did not receive the good or service you purchased if you didn't receive the item. If you use a credit card, the opposite is true; the company must prove that you did receive the good or service that you purchased.

Internet purchases are very safe and secure if you make the purchase with a reliable company. Somewhere on the screen you should see a closed padlock; this means the site is secure. Purchases on a credit card do not affect your checking account and therefore your cash flow. So, if the site is fraudulent, it at least happened on your credit card. Fraud on your debit card would affect the cash you have access to. In either case, you are not responsible to pay for the fraudulent purchases, however; you must notify your financial institution immediately. Of course, you should check with your financial institution for their policies and procedures in dealing with fraudulent purchases and what you are liable to pay, if anything. It's good to know these policies in advance for two reasons:
1. You won't stress as much over the situation if it happens to you because you at least know the process to go about rectifying the situation
2. If a bank's policies aren't protective of you, you may not want to bank with them at all

Online Banking

The most important tool any financial institution can provide their customers is online banking. Many basic customer service requests (changing your address and phone number) and transactions (credit card payments, transferring funds) can be completed online, saving you a trip to a banking center.

Some examples of the uses of online banking are:
- Change of Address/Phone Number/E-Mail Address
- View your account statement
- Place a stop payment on a check
- Reorder checks and deposit slips
- Set and manage alerts for your account
- Make credit card/loan payments from your checking account
- Transfer money between accounts
- Request a credit line increase on your credit card
- Pay bills with online bill pay

Online banking also offers up-to-the-minute balance information on your account, including recent purchases. If you go into a banking center, your recent credit card purchase may not reflect of the teller's system until the following business day. The reasoning behind this delay is a very technical one that deals the legality of which associates can see what information. For the sake of your knowledge, just know if you want up-to-the-minute information on your credit card check online banking. Notice, next time you call customer service, you speak to one specialist when dealing with your checking account and another person when dealing with your credit card. This is because of that very technical explanation of who can legally see what information.

Daily checking of online banking not only keeps you on top of your spending habits but it also is the best way for you to notice any fraudulent purchases that might have been made on your account. If you notice any fraudulent purchases on your account, contact the Fraud Department of your financial institution immediately.

Online banking is simple to navigate, but if you need assistance you are always more than welcome to go into a banking center and have someone show you how to use the most basic and more complicated features of this great tool.

Quicken, and other similar programs, offer you an electronic checkbook register which automatically updates with online banking. For the computer savvy, these tools can help you keep track of your spending accurately and also offers you tools and charts to see what exactly you are spending your money on. It would be worth the investment to buy this program or one like it if it can help you keep track of your spending or prevent you from overdrawing your account. The program must be connected to the Internet to stay updated with your online banking. I don't use a program like this, but I know others who swear by it.

Every bank carries checkbook registers (a log where you can track all of your transactions) and should give them to you for free. If you are unable to get a checkbook register from your financial institution, you can always create your own. This will keep you on top of your finances, ahead of the bank and help you not overspend.

You need to be constant and diligent about it though. Your handwritten checkbook is more accurate and more reliable than online banking. Every time you write a check, make a purchase, or do anything involving your account, put it into your checkbook. You don't want to forget about that $600 rent check you wrote and end up overdrawing your account. The bank won't know about any check you write until it posts to your account. This lack of knowledge is why online banking doesn't reflect a check as pending and why keeping a manual checkbook is vital. One other important note about checks: just because you have them doesn't mean you still have money in your account.

It's a good idea to stay diligent with online banking and your handwritten register to cross reference and catch mistakes. I say this because there is a chance that you can make an error in your calculations. After all, we are human. If your handwritten checkbook register matches with online banking, then you are good to go! You're balanced!

The bank is not your personal consultant; you will not be called when you overdraw your account to be told to deposit money. You should be responsible for your own account. The financial institution will inform you of a disturbance in your account through the mail. The natural delay that comes with standard mail is the exact reason you should be enrolled in automatic alerts with your account. Remember, banks make money every time you overdraw your account or spend more than your credit limit. Money for the bank means profit.

Many banks offer alerts to keep you in the know on your account. The most common are email and text alerts. Alerts inform you of:
- When your account balance goes below a certain dollar amount
- When a direct deposit is posts to your account
- When your account is overdrawn
- When a check posts to your account

There are also credit card alerts reminding you to make a payment. These can be helpful and possibly even prevent an overdraft from occurring. So go enroll!

Overdrafts

In banking, "credits" are posted to your account before "debits". This process simply states that money will post *into* your account first, then transactions that take money out will post second. For example, if you overspend and bring your account into the negative by $100 at around noon, as long as you deposit at least $100 by the end of the business day, you will not be assessed an overdraft fee.

One of the worst things that a person can do to their account and their relationship with the bank is to overdraw the account. Not only does overdrawing generate fees for you, but it also puts a bad mark on your account. This mark can be on your account for a year or more. Overdrawing makes you look irresponsible with your money. Sometimes life just happens and overdrawing cannot be avoided, so be prepared with overdraft protection!

Most, if not all, banks offer overdraft protection for free. Overdraft protection is a system set up to protect you from overdrawing your account. If you were to overspend in your checking account, overdraft protection will pull money from either a savings account or a credit line and automatically transfer those funds to your checking account to cover the negative amount. Thus, at the end of the day, your account will not be in the negative. Some banks charge a small fee for you to use overdraft protection ($5 to $10), but not always. In the end, a $10 fee is much better then being assessed multiple $35 fees. Overdraft protection is a smart idea, because the amount of money saved by you in overdraft fees makes overdraft protection more than worthwhile.

Overdraft fees are assessed in many ways:
- Each occurrence of an overdraft is one flat rate (i.e. $35 per occurrence).
- A tiered method is a progression where your first instances are low fee amounts then gradually get bigger the more times your overdraw, but are capped at a certain amount. For example, the first few overdrafts are at $19, and then overdrafts four through six are at $30, then every occurrence after six is at the highest amount of $40.
- Every day that your account is overdrawn a fee is assessed.
- A combination of per item occurrence and per day occurrence.

For overdraft protection, I recommend having your checking account linked with a line of credit/ credit card specifically for overdraft protection. This is the best way to go, because if there is no money in your savings account, the bank will not overdraw your savings in order to prevent your checking from being overdrawn. The same principle applies to credit well. If you don't have any available credit, then you will not be protected. In order to make sure you have available credit, I recommend that you have a credit card for your everyday spending and then a second line of credit/ credit card with a low limit ($500) that is activated and only used for overdraft protection.

Checks

When you open a checking account, you have the option to order checks. It is to your benefit to get the smallest and cheapest order possible. The main reason for this is so you can enroll in direct deposit with your employer. Often, employers require a voided check (a check with the word void written across it) to process your direct deposit request. I recommend getting the smallest order because in today's day and age, we don't really write checks that often, and if you do need to write a check, you most likely should be able to use online banking for it, and that would mean you don't actually have to write the check yourself. So don't waste your money on a big check order.

Some high school economics classes teach students how to write a check. Sometimes, a parent will teach their children how to write a check, but sadly, many people still don't know or haven't been taught correctly. While it's true that checks may soon be a thing of the past, they aren't entirely extinct from banking yet. Gifts and rent payments are given in check form still, so you aren't completely free from check writing.

Look at the example check below.

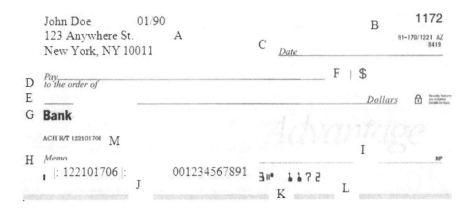

When looking at a check, there are many different parts to notice.

A- In the upper left corner is personal information: your name (and anyone else on your account) along with your address. Sometimes a phone number is also included.

B- In the upper right corner is the check number. Directly below the check number are a series of numbers and a state code. This is for internal banking use only, so don't worry about it.

C- Below that series of numbers is the space for you to put the date.

D- The next important part of a check is the "Pay to the Order of" line. When writing a check, it's best to spell the name of the person or business correctly. Furthermore, knowing the implications of what you write is vital. If a check is written to John Doe <u>or</u> Jane Doe, either party can cash or deposit the check. If a check is written to John Doe <u>and</u> Jane Doe, both parties must be present to negotiate the check. If a check is written to John Doe and/or Jane Doe, the *and* is dominant. The only exception is when the check is deposited into an account with both persons' names on it. If the check is written to both parties, then the check can only be deposited into an account with both parties listed as owners of the account. If John Doe wants to deposit the check into an account with only his name, he is not able to do so because Jane never had access to her funds. He would have to deposit the check into the account with both John and Jane Doe's name on it, and then transfer the funds to his private account. This policy makes it possible to prove (if there is a dispute) that both parties did receive their funds.

E- Below that is the line where you write out in words how much the check is worth. Example: One Hundred and 0/100. This is called the written amount.

F- To the right of that is where you write numerically how much the check is for. For example: 100.00. The handwritten and numeric amounts must match.

G- In our example check, below these two lines are the name, logo and information of the financial institution for the check.

H- The memo line is just a reference line for you. Some people write a little message, such as Happy Birthday, or you can place an account number there if making a payment.

I- The signature line on the bottom right is crucial. If this line isn't signed, the check is invalid and cannot be negotiated. The person who signs in this spot is the person who is writing the check, namely one of the people listed in the left hand corner. Another anti-fraud measure is the line itself. The line is actually the words "SIGNATURE ONLY" written in very tiny writing. If you receive a personal check (non-business check) that is just a line, then you *may* have a fraudulent check.

J- The very bottom of the check shows you a series of numbers. The bottom left between the smiley faces (|:) is the routing number. A routing number is a number used in the world of banking to identify the bank and the state that account was opened in. Therefore, a routing number is different from bank to bank, and different from state to state within the same bank.

K- The next series of numbers is your full account number.

L- After the account number will be your check number, written again. You can find the check number of any check in two places, the upper right hand corner and on the bottom. If receiving a check and those two numbers don't match, you may have a fraudulent check.

M- Your routing number, listed again.

Endorsing a Check

When receiving a check, you must endorse the check as it is written to you. To endorse a check, you just sign the back. You are taking responsibility for the check and telling the bank that there are funds to support the check. If the funds aren't there, you are agreeing to have the funds taken out of your account along with a fee. When you process that check, you are stating that the check is valid and there are no problems with it. If there are any problems, you, as the endorser, will be responsible for any fees incurred. It's unfair that you have to deal with the problems associated with someone writing you a bad check, but that's how it is.

If you normally go by Jack Moore, but your real name is John Moore on your account and the check is written to Jack Moore, you must endorse the check as Jack (as it is written to you) then endorse the check as John Moore (how it is on your account) below. If the check is written to you as John D. Moore, then you MUST endorse the check with your middle initial, even if your middle initial isn't in your name with the bank. The check must be endorsed EXACTLY how it is written to you.

It is always acceptable to over endorse a check, like signing as Susan Raye Crane if the check is written to Susan Crane. It is not acceptable to under endorse a check, signing Susan when the check is written to Susan Crane.

If there is no line or box for you to endorse the check on the back, the industry asks that you endorse the check on the backside on the same end as where the payer's name and address are written. If you are unsure on how or where to endorse the check, ask the teller at your bank.

Processing a Check

When you present a check to a teller, they will most likely scan the check. The MICR machine reads the line of numbers on the bottom of the check. MICR stands for Magnetic Ink Character Recognition. All checks have the account number and routing number written in MICR ink. When checks are scanned, the machine is able to read the account number, but only if it is written in MICR ink. As an added security only real checks can be read by this machine, which is why making sure the entire check is intact when you present it to a teller is vital. If any part of the MICR line is missing from a check, the check is invalid and non-negotiable. The MICR numbers are an anti-fraud measure and are one of many ways of proving that a check is real and valid. Banks scan the MICR line and their systems automatically can process the check. The MICR tells the computer systems what state the check came from, which bank the check came from, and the account number and check number of the account it is coming from.

There is a myth that future dating your check—writing a check with a date set in the future—is a way to float your funds. It doesn't work. While a check is not negotiable until the date written on the check, banks are still able to process the check, which may cause you to overdraw your account. The simple reason for this is, a teller could misread the date. A good rule about check writing (and credit card purchases, for that matter) is that if you don't have the money, don't write the check. If you write a check and it is returned for insufficient funds, you look irresponsible in the eyes of the bank, and also the person you wrote the check to.

In banking, there is something called a third party check. A third party check is a check that is written by one person (the payer) being paid to another person (the payee), but a third party is trying to negotiate it.

For example, your friend John's mother (the payer) wrote John (the payee) a check, and *you* try and go to the bank to cash it. Third party checks are highly susceptible to fraud. Though your friend John may have signed the back of the check and signed it over to you, it doesn't mean that the bank will honor it. For all that anyone knows, you could have stolen the check, forged John's signature, and then presented it to the bank. In an extreme case scenario, John could claim that he never got the money from his check. His mom would prove that he did since the money would have left her account. Both John and his mom would then contact the bank. After the bank does research, they trace the check back to you. John can then take you to court and send you to prison for check fraud. I am not saying this will happen, but it could. Is it really worth it?

Your friend John should get his own account and negotiate his own checks in it. If he doesn't have an account, refer him to wherever you bank. Most banks offer bonuses to people who personally refer new customers to them (around $25 per person usually). You and your friend are both following the law and getting money for it!

ID Requirements

ID requirements set forth by your financial institution are for your protection. You wouldn't want them to just give your money away to anyone would you? It is always a good rule to carry your bankcard with you (your debit card, credit card or ATM card) and a non-expired government-issued state ID, permit, driver's license or passport. Some banks offer photos for your debit and credit cards. This additional security feature should be free and allows you to have a primary picture ID with the bank. I highly recommend getting the photo, since the photo might also prevent fraud on your account if your card is stolen. Large transactions generally require two forms of valid ID. Many people claim that they don't have two IDs, but everyone definitely does. Two IDs are required to open the account, so you could easily use those. Then, once the account is opened, you get an additional ID in the form of your check card or ATM card.

Just a note, if your ID is expired it is **invalid** and the bank may not accept it as proper identification in order to let you process transactions

I must emphasize that you do not get angry with a teller when they ask you for identification. It is for YOUR security and protection. Even if you have seen that teller before, and they KNOW it's you, it doesn't matter. Each transaction requires ID, so give it to them. I liked my job at the bank much more than breaking the rules for a customer who wasn't prepared. I could be fired for that sort of rule breaking.

If you ever plan on taking out a large sum of cash (generally over $5,000), it is not only courteous but requested that you give the specific banking center where you are withdrawing the funds from notice of the withdrawal if you need a certain denomination of bills. Notifying the banking center allows them to order extra cash to take care of your request. Though it is a bank, banks are only allowed to carry a certain amount of cash on hand in each banking center. A large withdrawal, especially wanting all of the bills in one denomination, may not be possible without advance notice. Two to three business days should be enough time.

If you bank with the financial institution you are taking the money out of, you can always opt for a cashier's check. This is a check that has guaranteed funds. For example, instead of buying that used car from your neighbor with $6300 in cash, you can present him with a cashier's check you obtained from your local banking center. The funds are available immediately and there is no chance that the check will be returned for insufficient funds because the check is paid for up front. When going to the bank to purchase a cashier's check, you must come prepared with the correct spelling of the person or business it is going to. Some banks charge fees for bank checks (Money Orders and Cashiers Checks) which could range from $1 all the way up to $20, so keep that in mind when you go to purchase a bank check.

Some banks offer both cashier's checks and money orders. Money orders generally don't go above a certain dollar amount ($500 or $1000 for example). Cashier's checks can be for any dollar amount. Both money orders and cashier's checks are guaranteed and paid for up-front.

There is one caveat to cashier's checks. In the end, a cashier's check is a check. Cashier's checks are guaranteed up to $5,000 immediately according to banking regulation CC, but any amount above this threshold is subject to a hold if the check is drawn off of another financial institution. A hold would be placed on a cashier's check for the same reason a hold would be placed on a personal check, due to the amount of the deposit and your relationship with your financial institution so the funds can be verified. The reason a hold may still be placed is because the check could still be fraudulent or have a stop payment placed on it.

Cashing Checks

Cashing a check at a bank where you are not a customer is a courtesy. If the bank allows you to cash a check, you may not get to choose how you get your money back. For example, if you want all $100 bills and they happen to be running low, they will keep hundreds for their customers and give you fifties and twenties instead, There may even be a check-cashing fee. You have no right to demand they do something for you, since you are not one of their customers. Remember, a teller's cash is for their customers not you, the non-customer.

Fraud is the main reason banks refuse to cash checks for non-customers. If the check is fraudulent, the bank has no way of recouping the money lost. Yes, the check is drawn off of the bank you are in and they have the ability to cash it, but it doesn't mean that the bank will. Since they aren't legally required to, sometimes they won't. Banks are looking after themselves and their customers first.

Keep this next tidbit in mind: you can't cash a check at a bank where you are not a customer if the check you are cashing is not from that bank. For example, you cannot go to Bank B (as a non-customer) and ask to cash a check drawn off of Bank C if you don't have an account there. You have no account to back up the funds if it comes back insufficient, and Bank B has no way to verify the funds are even in that account since it isn't drawn off of them. So go to your bank, Bank A, and negotiate the check.

7
Savings Accounts

Put the SAVY in Saving

CONGRATULATIONS ON GETTING A SAVINGS ACCOUNT. This is the first step to start saving money for your future, whether it's near or distant. So why should you save your money? I save money in case there is an emergency and I need the extra cash. I also save money to make future, short-term goal purchases (a new iPod, moving into a new apartment and needing a security deposit, buying a new cell phone, buying a new laptop, etc.). My long-term savings goals include saving money for a house, a new car and my retirement. I currently have an IRA into which I make monthly contributions to start saving for my retirement. Yes, it's years away, but compound interest can only work to my benefit. For some, they can make a nice living by saving a bulk of cash and earning large sums of interest, thus supplementing their income.

Experts say the best mindset to have in order to save is PYF—Pay Yourself First. To accomplish this, experts advise figuring out your total net income, and consider 10% of your net income as a bill to yourself. If it's a bill, you have to pay it, but instead of it going to some big corporation, it's going to the most important business in your life: You, Inc. If you get into the habit of paying yourself first every month, saving will be easy. While in theory this sounds great, in actuality, many teenagers will spend any leftover money they have. My personal advice is to save as much as you can and to enroll your savings account with direct deposit. If you don't see the money or actually hold it in your hand, the loss of pocket money is less tangible. When saving becomes routine, you no longer view it as a loss of income. In the end, it's about discipline.

When my bills were limited and I was living at home, I put the majority of my income into my savings account. I deposited into my checking account enough to pay bills and give myself a little pocket cash allowing me to get in the habit of saving because the rest of the money went into my savings account.

The money I saved allowed me to purchase:
- A car
- iPod
- Digital camera
- Laptop
- Afford moving to New York City
- Create an emergency fund if I fell onto hard times.

The more you get into the habit of saving, the easier it will be to manage your money.

What's the Difference?

A checking account and a savings account are very different.

A checking account:
- Is the primary account people use.
- Has unlimited deductions from the account fee free.
- Has checks, which are slips of specialized paper that takes place of cash in processing a monetary transaction.
- Has a debit card, which allows you to make a purchase anywhere a card is accepted, as well as providing access to cash for purchases and ATM withdrawals.
- Generally is a non-interest bearing account (it earns no interest)

A savings account:
- Earns interest on the principal within the account.
- Is limited in the number of debits that can post to the account within one statement cycle.
- Has an ATM card, which allows you access to your savings account from an ATM only.

Your debit card can grant you access to your savings for ATM withdrawals, but cannot be linked as the main account in which debit transactions are processed.

What's in it for me?

The main reason to fund a savings account is that you earn money off of the cash in the account. This earned money is called interest. I'm not going to lie; interest rates offered by major financial institutions leave something to be desired. Interest rates can range anywhere from .05% to .50% annually. So unless you plan on depositing a major sum of money into the savings account, you won't be making big returns. This grim reality generally keeps people from even getting a savings account. My personal belief is that *some* money is better than making *no* money at all.

Now that you are earning interest (or paying interest if you have a loan), there is a byproduct called compound interest, which must be explained. Interest is accrued every statement cycle and then placed into your account. On your next statement cycle, your balance plus the interest you have accrued thus far will earn interest..

Compound interest happens automatically, and works to your advantage in a savings situation. However, interest can work against you when you are paying back a loan or line of credit.

Time is key to compound interest. The longer you have the money in your account, the more money you will make through compounding. Regular deposits into the account help as well. Put money away now and allow both regular deposits and compound interest to work for you and help you save up for college, a car, a house or retirement.

Benefits of Saving

If you have your savings account with the same financial institution as your checking account, there are four major ways to save money and help you achieve your financial goals.

1. Automatic transfers from checking to savings
2. No monthly maintenance fees
3. Overdraft protection
4. Automatic saving through Keep The Change and other similar programs

You not only get the convenience of banking in one place, but with automatic transfers, a pre-determined amount of money is directly transferred from your checking to your savings account at the same time every month. This is good way to get into the habit of paying yourself first every month.

Another form of an automatic savings plan is to enroll your savings account in direct deposit. This way, every time you get paid, either a certain amount or a certain percentage of your net pay goes directly into your savings. You can do as much or as little as you want; the main goal is to save whatever you can afford. The more you save, the more you earn.

Many financial institutions offer a free savings account if you have a checking with them. Finding a savings account with no monthly maintenance fees will help you save your hard-earned money.

You can use your savings account for overdraft protection for your checking account. A savings account used for overdraft protection only works if you keep money in the account. If you don't plan on keeping a steady balance in the account (at least $500), then you should think about getting a credit card for overdraft protection. No matter which way you get overdraft protection, in the end, it saves you money on overdraft fees.

Bank of America offers a unique and one-of-a-kind savings program called Keep The Change. This program allows you to save money every time you use your Bank of America Check Card. For every purchase you make, the amount is rounded up to the nearest dollar; the difference is then transferred from your checking to your savings account. Bank of America also matches a certain percentage of the funds transferred on an annual basis. You receive your matching contributions into your savings account, and the program is free. It's not a lot of money, but it could be potentially a great way to save some money if you happen to use your debit card often.

Wells Fargo offers a similar program where, after every debit card purchase, they transfer $1 form your checking to your savings account. This gives you the opportunity to save more than with Bank of America's Keep The Change.

CDs!

A certificate of deposit (commonly referred to as a CD) is a type of savings/ investment account. When you invest money in a CD, you are essentially loaning the bank your money. While the bank has your money, it's theirs, and you don't have access to those funds until it matures and the CD term is over. Every CD has a defined length of time of how long the bank will keep your money. When that time is up, the CD has matured and the money is yours. The trade-off with a CD is: though your money is inaccessible (generally) you get a higher interest rate than a regular savings account. Plus your interest compounds!

Banks offer CDs because the money they receive is taken and invested on behalf of the bank. When banks invest, they more often than not make large returns and big profits on their investment. A small portion of what banks earn is the interest paid to you.

Though CDs are an investment, you are guaranteed to get your original investment back with interest. CDs are FDIC insured, which is why a CD is a good investment, because you won't lose any money. Because there is a low risk in investing in a CD, there is a low reward. While you are guaranteed to make money, you could potentially make more money in a higher risk investment, such as the stock market. High risk reaps high rewards. CDs are a great way to play it safe.

CD terms—meaning how long the money is being used by the bank— vary. The longer the bank holds onto your funds, the higher the interest rate and the more compounding works for you. Some banks offer short-term CDs (four months for example) as well as long-term CDs (96 months for example). CD rates vary based on the economy, the federal interest rate and per financial institution.

When a CD reaches its maturity date, your financial institution will notify you in advance so you can plan your next step.

What are my options when my CD matures?

- Cash out the CD and use the money as you wish
- Allow the money to be rolled over into a new CD for the same term and rate
- Cash out the CD and go somewhere else for a better CD rate or term
- Cash out the CD and reinvest the principal and do with the interest what you wish

With every rule there is an exception. Money invested in CDs is locked away, however, in certain situations you are able to withdraw funds before the maturity date. There most likely will be a fee for early withdrawal, so make sure the withdrawal is for an emergency.

Some banks may offer a flexible CD in which, after a predetermined amount of time, you are able to take a withdrawal out of your CD without paying any fees. A personal banker would be the best person to speak to in a banking center about the different kinds of CDs that a particular financial institution offers.

Online Savings

If you don't want to lock your money away by investing in a CD, but you still want a higher interest rate with the liquidity of a financial institution's savings account, you might consider an online savings account. Online savings accounts require you to have a checking account with a traditional financial institution, which is great because that means you don't have to switch banks! The reason you must have a traditional account is because in order to put money into the online savings account, the online bank electronically debits the money from your checking to credit the savings, just like an automatic payment. Since it is an *online* savings account, you can't go into a banking center to do a deposit; the funds must be transferred online through the ACH (Automated Clearing House).

The benefit of an online savings account is an increase in savings because of higher interest rates. Online banks are able to offer higher interest rates because they don't have as much overhead and administrative costs as traditional banks. With no banking centers (and subsequent electric bills, maintenance, and payroll costs) and no limit on where an account can be opened, the online bank is able to cut costs and pass the savings on to you.

I would recommend keeping the bulk of your savings in an online savings account because of the higher interest rates, and keep only limited funds in a traditional bank's savings account.

I manage my money this way: I keep the bulk of my savings in my online account. Every month I place my money for bills into my traditional savings account. I do this because the money I make at the beginning of the month immediately goes to my bills. For the most part, it sits there for a few weeks, so I might as well have it in a savings account to earn some money. At the end of the month, when I need the money, I make one big transfer from my savings to my checking using my free online banking. I also don't want to get rid of my traditional savings account because it's the account I have had the longest with that bank, thus maintaining my long relationship.

Since the funds are being processed over the Internet, funds availability isn't instantaneous in an online savings account. It can take anywhere between 5 to 10 business days for the money to post into the online savings account, and anywhere between 1 to 5 business days for the funds to post into your checking account. The funds aren't as readily available as going into a banking center and withdrawing cash, but you are receiving more money in interest and a no-fee account. In theory, this shouldn't be a problem. If you know you will be making a big purchase, then you can schedule the transfer of funds in enough time to make sure it's available when needed.

Referral Bonus

Like a traditional financial institution, online banks pay their customers for referring new customers to them. Check with friends and family about which online bank they use if they have one. You could then use them as a referral and both you and your friend will get a bonus. If no one close to you has an online account, start the trend. Start an account for yourself and refer your friends and family and help them achieve their financial goals—and earn money in the process.

Ways to Save

One technique to help you save money is to have a clear goal for why you are saving. If you are saving just to save, you see no point in doing it and have no motivation to do it. If you have a clear reason to save, it will be much easier. Need a new laptop before you go off to college? Forced into paying your own way through college? Looking to get an apartment of your own? How about that new car you wanted to get?

Having a rainy day fund is also a good idea. A rainy day fund is simply having enough money in your savings account to where you could completely survive off of those funds for a certain period of time. Many recommend for adults in careers to have a six to nine month emergency fund. Obviously, we can't afford that, so do what makes sense for you and your lifestyle. Adulthood is expensive, and having a clear reason as to why you are saving will give you a sense of accomplishment when you do reach your goals. Most experts say that you should only put money into a traditional savings account if the money you are putting in there will be used for a purchase within the next five years. If your goals are to purchase something beyond 5 years, you should look to other forms of saving or investment (either a CD or the stock market, potentially). I agree with this completely. If you know you won't need a chunk of cash, then locking it away in a CD to earn interest is a great idea. Make your money work for you. Be careful of the stock market, because those investments aren't FDIC insured. If the market crashes, you could lose all of the money you invested.

Technical Stuff

Savings accounts are designed for money to go in more often than out. With this mindset all banks must adhere to a federal guideline. A customer can only take money out of a savings account up to three times per statement cycle (six times if it's a money market savings account). The fee is small, but the bank charges you every time you surpass your limit. Again, this is a federal, not an individual financial institution fee, which is supposed to deter you from taking money out of your savings account too often. When you open a savings account, you agree to follow federal guidelines. To compensate for this inconvenience, you earn interest on money put away into a savings account. If you plan on using the money soon after depositing it into your savings account or plan on making multiple withdrawals, put the money into your checking account instead.

If you need to access money in a savings account, take out a big chunk; use what you need, then redeposit the remainder back into your savings. If you take money out multiple times from your savings you will incur a fee, but if you only withdraw once, then there is no fee. Remember, you can do unlimited deposits. Savings accounts are primarily for you to put money in. Money should only be taken out for either emergencies or a big purchase.

8

Credit Cards
and Other Lines of Credit

IN ORDER TO MAKE A BIG PURCHASE IN AMERICA such as a car or home, you need to have credit unless you can pay for these things with cash. The only way to have good credit is to build it, and the only way to build good credit is to go into debt. There are many ways to build good credit, but remember that good credit can take a lifetime to build and only a day to decimate.

Givin' You Some Credit

Now, don't let the following information scare you. You can still have fun with your credit card if you use it wisely. Knowing the downfalls and the traps of credit cards gives you the advantage to think ahead and not drown in debt. Because, the reality of it is, life happens, and sometimes you just don't have the money you need saved.

Credit Card Basics

In the world of credit cards, there are four major brands: Visa, MasterCard, Discover and American Express. If one of these logos aren't on your card, it probably isn't a credit card.

Debt to Credit Ratio

One important factor in deciding whether or not to extend credit to someone is his or her debt ratio. I will go into what makes up your FICO score later, but for now, just know that your debt ratio makes up 30% of your FICO Credit Score. While there is no magic ratio percentage that gives you perfect credit, it is true that the lower the ratio, the better. The key is to find the right balance between debt and how much credit you have available to you. 10% is better than 15%, but 15% is better than 20%. Under 20% is preferred.

Here are two examples of the debt ratios.

Person A

	Debt (Balance)	Credit Limit
Credit Card One	$2000	$3000
Credit Card Two	$3000	$7000

Person B

	Debt (Balance)	Credit Limit
Credit Card One	$1500	$5000
Credit Card Two	$500	$5000

Each person has $10,000 in total credit available to him or her. Person A is 50% in debt while Person B is only 20% in debt. While 20% is better than 50%, 50% is also better than 60%.

I would recommend having two or three credit cards that are active in your name at all times. Once you have these cards, don't get more. If you do get another card, eliminate another one. One should be for everyday use, one for overdraft protection, and one for emergencies. As you find the perfect card, you don't need to get more. Stick with the ones you have and you will see, over time, your rate may lower and your limit may increase. Longevity is crucial in building credit.

Keep in mind that when you close an account, it will affect your debt to credit ratio. Your debt level is the same before you closed out the card, but now your available credit has decreased once the card is closed, thus increasing your debt ratio (which isn't good).

As you start building your credit, you may rotate through different cards until you find the right fit. That's fine. It's good to get these bumps out of the way now rather than later. Once you do find the right mix of cards, stay with it. Why fix something that isn't broken?

My number one rule for credit cards: if you don't have the money to pay for it, then you can't afford it. If you live by this rule, you will be one step closer to living a debt-free life. Of course there are exceptions to this rule, such as a big purchase that is necessary. For example: a laptop, bed, or student loans. If you make a big purchase, then make a payment plan or a goal of when to pay the balance off and stick to it! I know that it is a lot easier to say this and that the actual implementation of this advice is difficult, but it can be done. You have to fight the allure to buy now and pay later, because when you pay later, you paid more for your item than the original sale price. And if you don't stick to a realistic repayment plan, you'll drown in debt.

<u>Wants versus Needs</u>

In order to help you decide what to purchase on credit (or what to buy in general; really), you need to ask yourself a simple question. Is this purchase a *need* or a *want*? A need is something that is essential to your livelihood. A want is a material item that you really want for whatever reason, but *could* live without.

Needs include:
- Food/groceries
- Clothes for work
- Rent and utility bills
- Gas/public transit fare to get to and from work and school
- A laptop for school (I'll let you splurge and get a Mac)
- A bed to sleep on

Wants include:
- Buying name brands over generic brands
- Buying new name-brand sunglasses
- A flat-screen TV
- Taking a cab
- Computer games
- Eating out at restaurants and ordering take-out
- Manicures and pedicures
- Tanning
- New bags, clothes, and accessories
- Going to the bar

Small purchases here and there add up quickly, so you must use self-constraint and caution when it comes to spending money.

Building Credit

If you don't want a credit card, you have other options to build your credit. When you move out of your parents' house, you become responsible for everything they used to pay for. These kinds of expenses will also help establish credit:

- Utilities (gas, electric, water)
- Cable (TV)
- Cell phone
- Internet
- Student loans
- Car payment
- Car insurance

Because your bills can and will impact your credit, you need to pay them on time. You can pay most of them automatically with your credit card, which means you will never be late and you can start racking up points on that credit card! If you don't have a credit card, you can also do automatic payments and deductions from your checking account. Be careful though, Regulation E will allow your account to overdraw because of an automatic payment, which could cause overdraft fees.

When I worked at a restaurant in the Flatiron district of Manhattan, the chef told me he was always late paying his bills, yet he had plenty of money to pay them. He just kept forgetting to send in the checks. While this is very possible, it's still no excuse. I recommended to him that he enroll in automatic bill pay so he pays his bills on time and his credit is no longer negatively affected. I recommend the same to you. You can't be lazy in life. You just can't be.

I personally pay all bills possible with my credit card. I'm earning points and since I have to spend that money anyway, I might as well get something for it. At the time the bill is charged to my credit card, I transfer the funds from my checking to my credit card in the form of a payment. Thus, I pay no interest on these bills. If I can't pay automatically on my credit card, I have the bill automatically debited from my checking account.

There is a downside to getting bills in just your name. Without a co-signer or a credit history, you will have to pay higher interest rates, premiums, and sometimes even put down a security deposit. Unfortunately, there is no way around this. You just need to stick it out, and once you have a healthy credit score, then you can work on lowering your rate or premium. In the world of credit, you have to prove yourself.

If you drive, then car insurance is another way of impacting your credit rating. Your main goal is to show creditors that you can be trusted to borrow money and pay it back. Since longevity is crucial to building and sustaining a healthy credit score, keep bills in your name and pay them on time. Longevity accounts for 15% of what makes up your credit score.

When a mobile phone service provider issues a cell phone, you sign a contract. The contract states you will pay your bill, on time, every month. If you don't, the contract outlines the consequences. As your relationship builds with the provider, the company will continue to report payment history and habits to the credit bureaus, thus changing your credit score and credit history. For your first contract, you probably don't have a credit history, which means you will probably have to put a security deposit down in order to get service.

Student loans—such as the federally subsidized Stafford loan—are in your name and therefore affect your credit rating. The loan accrues interest every month, which the government pays until six months after you graduate. This is good because you will have a loan on your credit history beginning when you start school that is paid on time every month while you are enrolled in school at least part time. You don't start paying until after you graduate. Of course, do not get a loan if you don't need it and *always* pay your loans on time.

Best Card for YOU!

When you enter the world of credit and credit building there are many factors to take into account before deciding on a particular line of credit.

You won't have an official credit history and no credit history means you are considered a higher risk to a credit card company. What does all of that mean to you? Well, it means you will have a higher interest rate than those with a good credit history. A higher interest rate means you are paying more money to the banks.

Here are some things to consider:

What's the APR? The first factor in deciding on a credit card is the APR (Annual Percentage Rate). The APR is the percentage used to calculate the interest you will pay on purchases you make. You obviously want the lowest APR you can get, especially if you plan on carrying a balance from month to month. The longer you hold a balance on your card, the more money you will pay in interest.

If you keep a balance on your card for more than a month, you will be subjected to the effects of compounding interest. What does this mean to you? You are spending more money in interest, which means you are spending more money paying off your original purchase than what your original purchase actually cost. You're paying interest on interest.

So, if your APR is 15%, then over the course of the year, you will have paid an amount in interest equal to 15% of your total purchases. Now, if you look at your credit card statement, you will notice that your APR is broken down into a daily percentage rate. This daily percentage rate is the rate at which your balance is charged interest daily, which by the end of the month totals 1.25% (or 1/12 of your APR). The amount you actually pay will be dictated by your APY, or Annual Percentage Yield, which is essentially the rate that you payback interest when you factor in compound interest. If you pay off your credit card every month, you avoid paying interest.

Is the card a rewards card? Most credit cards offer rewards. With them you earn points, which can be redeemed for prizes, cash back, or air travel. For every $1 you spend, you get a point. You can even pay your bills with the credit card to start earning points quicker. Most cards start offering redemption around 2500 points. Generally, a reward you get for this low amount in points is something along the lines of a $5 gift card somewhere. If you get enough points, you can purchase an airline ticket for the vacation you are planning, and maybe even reduce the price on the hotel you are staying at. With rewards points, taking that trip to Salt Lake City during the winter to go snow boarding is now at least somewhat possible. Balance transfers and cash advances are generally exempt from the points program, but you will need to check with your bank on that.

Does the financial institution offer photo security for your credit card account? Is your photo on the actual card? Photo security is a great deterrent for fraud. Photo security credit cards are similar to their debit card counterparts. Check back in the checking chapter for more information.

Is the card a co-branded credit card? A co-branded credit card is a credit card that is offered in conjunction between a company or charity and a particular financial institution with the logo of the company or cause on the actual card. A popular co-branded credit card would be an airlines card, where a particular bank offers the credit card for a particular airline, but the face of the card is the logo of that particular airline. If you have a co-branded credit card, instead of your points going into a pool where you choose what you can redeem your points for, all of your points go towards one common reward, miles for a flight. Co-branded cards make your rewards more specific and their interest rates are generally higher than an average credit card.

A normal points card gives you the option to choose what you want to get with your points (cash back, hotel room, new iPod, etc). You will need to evaluate what is important to you and make a decision. Do you live far from home? Could you benefit from earning airline tickets to travel? Do you want a lower interest rate?

You pay the bank with a co-branded credit card, not the company, generally. For example, I have a Delta American Express Credit Card; I pay American Express, not Delta. If you get a department store credit card, however, you should be able to make credit card payments at a department store's location.

Getting a Credit Card

Credit cards are a great tool in building an individual's credit if used correctly. A credit card is offered either directly through a crediting company that specializes in extending lines of credit (Visa, MasterCard, American Express and Discover) or by a financial institution. Credit cards offered by a financial institution are insured by one of the four credit companies listed above.

There are many ways to get a credit card:
1) You can go to a credit card issuer and apply directly with them. This method is most common.
2) Pre-approval credit card offers via mail solicitation.
3) Pre-approval credit card based on your relationship with your financial institution.

In the first scenario, you apply for a credit card directly with the company issuing you the credit card. I would recommend going to the place where you bank and apply for your credit card there, but only if you are happy with the other banking services they provide you. This act shows loyalty and it also allows you to bank all in one place. In order to apply you will see a personal banker who collects information about you and pulls your credit report and FICO credit score. Based on your score, the bank will review the risk of offering you credit and either reject or accept your application. You can also apply online.

If you are rejected for a credit card, work on improving your credit score. Your next step could be to either get a secured credit card or find a credit card company who targets people who don't have the best credit. If you know you have horrible credit, this may be a place where you can start building and correcting your credit problem. You will be charged a higher interest rate, but it's a step in the right direction. Improve your score and either get a new card with a better rate or have your current rate lowered.

If you are young and in school, get one credit card to start off with. Apply for a bank's most basic card or their student credit card. There are no perks with these cards, but it's a step in the right direction.

A normal credit card is an unsecured loan. If you don't pay, the bank cannot force you to sell anything in order to pay back your debts. In the case of a mortgage, however, your home is the security for the bank. If you don't pay your mortgage, the bank will take ownership of your house.

A secured credit card is a credit card, but you pay a security deposit upfront. The amount of the deposit will generally be the card's limit. For example, you put down a $300 security deposit and you have a $300 credit limit. You charge purchases to your card, and you pay it off in time, just like a regular card. After a year, you should be able to convert your secured credit card to an unsecured credit card, and receive your deposit back. The reason you put the deposit down upfront is in case you don't pay. If you don't make a payment or are late on a payment, then the bank gets to keep your full security deposit.

Pros of Secured Credit Cards
- Start building credit
- Prove yourself worthy of credit

Cons of Secured Credit Cards
• Have to put money down upfront
• Credit limit based on the amount of your security deposit

The second scenario begins once you turn 21. Upon your 21ˢᵗ birthday, you will most likely start getting pre-approval credit card offers in the mail. They are credit card companies who target young adults and try to set them up with credit. I warn you, I think this is very dangerous and one of the reasons so many young adults are in financial trouble. It is nonetheless legal, and it's the nature of the beast. This recently changed from 18 to 21 after Congress passed credit card reform legislation.

Recent changes in credit practices also now makes it mandatory for anyone applying for a credit card between the ages of 18 and 21 to have a co-singer in order to get a credit card. The reasoning is, this co-signer will help the 18 year-old stay on top of their finances and teach them the monetary lessons they have yet to learn. It also prevents kids who are on their own for the first time from getting multiple cards and drowning in debt. Also, the co-signor can tell the young adult "no." The only exception to this rule is if the applicant has had a steady job for two to three years. Then, they are allowed to apply on their own. The credit card company will then decide if they want to extend credit to the applicant or not. So it's still possible to be 18 and have your own credit card.

The interest rates on these pre-approvals are generally high, but most of your offers will be because you don't have credit history yet. If you choose to accept one of these offers, make sure you read all of the fine print before accepting. Check to see if there are any fees (annual fee, late payment fee, overage limit fee), if it is a rewards card, and what the credit limit is. Accepting one of these offers may be the best way to get your first credit card if a financial institution declined you. But remember, it's money you will have to pay back. If you miss a payment or pay late, not only will you be charged a fee, and be charged interest on that fee, but your interest rate could increase.

The third scenario comes directly through your bank. Your financial institution might pre-approve you for a credit card based on your relationship as a customer with the bank. These offers are generally geared towards pleasing you, their already existing customer, and are much better offers than pre-approvals in the mail. These offers, however, are sporadic and can't be relied upon to start your credit history with.

It's really up to you to research and find the best company for you. Luckily, in today's day and age, and being part of the Internet generation, we have a lot of resources that are all just a mouse click away. A popular website is BankRate, which can be found at www.bankrate.com. At this website you can compare and contrast all sorts of financial products.

To opt out of receiving pre-approval credit card offers in the mail, you can go to *__https://www.optoutprescreen.com.__* To opt out of pre-approvals from your financial institution, you need to speak to one of their customer service specialists. Opting out only lasts for 5 years, so every 5 years you will have to opt out again.

Good reasons to opt out are:
- Reduces junk mail
- Reduces risk of getting your identity stolen
- Helps the environment.
- Eliminates temptation of applying for another card

9

Debt

CREDIT CARDS ARE A NICE TOOL TO HELP YOU ACQUIRE what you want in life. Beware though: credit cards perpetuate society's need for instant gratification. If you can't control yourself, credit cards can become a nightmare.

Getting into Debt

You never want to pay just the minimum payment on your credit card every month; if you do, it will take you years to pay back your debt. By the time you have paid the card off, you will have paid much more in interest than the original principal due.

In order to get out of debt one must sacrifice certain luxuries in life. You won't be able to go out every weekend or pamper yourself every week because you don't have the money to do so. That's how you, or your friends, maxed out their credit card to begin with. To get out of debt, you will have to work extra hard, make larger payments and learn from your mistakes. As you pay off your debt, your credit score will improve. With an improved credit score you can get a credit card with a lower interest rate than the one you have, transfer the balance over, and pay off the same principal at a lower rate.

There are 30 days to a month, which is how long your statement cycle is for your credit card and loan accounts.

Want to hear a way to save on interest? Let's say that your credit card payment is always due at the end of the month. Instead of making your minimum payment at the end of the month when the payment is due, take your minimum payment, split it in half, and pay half (or more) now and half (or more) later. For example, if your minimum payment is $350 due on the 28th of every month, pay $175 early in the month and $175 later on.

Why should you do that? You will be paying less in interest because your daily balance will be lower later in the month. This will end up saving you money in interest in the long run. Applying this knowledge to any kind of loan could help you save hundreds of dollars. You won't see the results instantly, but you will be shaving years off of your repayment term and hundreds or thousands on dollars in future payments.

Another payment method to reduce interest payments and to pay off your loan faster is to take one month's payment, divide by 12, then add that amount to your monthly payment. You are now making 13 full payments in a 12-month span. For example, if your loan payment is $1,200 a month, paying just an extra $100 or more every month could help you shave off years on your payback period. If your student loans are based on you paying back the loan over 20 years, this method could help you reduce not only how much interest you pay, but also how many years you are paying as well. The shorter the loan term, the less time you are subjected to compound interest and the more money you will save.

There are many ways to make a payment. You can:
- Set up an automatic debit from your checking account
- Use online bill pay

- Go into a banking center and make the payment with a teller
- Mail in a check with a payment coupon to the bank

The above order is my preference in how I would recommend you make payments on anything, but you need to find what is best for you.

In regards to paying off debt, I personally pay the minimum amount due on all of my bills immediately upon receipt of the bill. I do this for a few reasons:

1. A major portion of your FICO Credit Score (35%) is based on paying all of your bills on time. Paying the bill as soon as you get it means you won't forget to pay it later. More on your FICO score later.
2. I won't be assessed a late fee. I don't know about you, but I don't have $40 lying around to just give to the bank. Generally, when people don't pay their bill, they don't have the money for it, so I'm pretty sure they also don't have money for the fee.
3. Anything I can do to help reduce the amount I owe in interest is a great idea to me.

Once I pay the minimum due I am in the clear. I can always pay more towards the principal later, but I am at least set for the month.

I don't believe credit cards are evil, but late fees and the effects of a missed payment on your interest rate and credit can seem like a death omen from the devil himself. So trust me, I understand why people call them evil. Here's an example. You get a promotional rate of 4.99% fixed for one year on balance transfers on a credit card. If you pay late on one of these payments, your interest rate jumps to 24% or higher for all future payments. Sometimes, the interest rate jump will retroactively apply to your balance from when the promotion began.

According to recent legislation, all financial institutions should give you ample notice before they increase your interest rate, at least 45 days.

But, if the notice of increase is in the original terms and conditions for the promotion, then that could be considered as giving you enough notice. Also, there is a push for more clarity in loan agreements so you are aware, before applying for the credit card or loan, of the repercussions of a missed or late payment.

On top of these interest rate hikes, you will also be charged a fee for a missed or late payment, which is more money you probably don't have which you now have to pay back with interest. Always pay your minimum due as soon as you get the bill then pay more at your leisure and don't worry about these interest rate hikes!

In order to make sure I have enough money to pay for all of my bills and not accidentally spend it, I have a separate account I use just for bills. This account is my savings account, so I can earn interest while my money is sitting in the bank. I calculate the amount I owe in bills every month, and then as I start making money, I deposit the funds into my savings account. Once I have enough money in there to cover all of my bills, I start putting the rest of my money into my checking account for personal spending. Since all of my bills come out around the same time, before the first bill is due, I make one big lump sum transfer online from my savings to my checking account. Anything left over at the end of the month is applied to my credit card, student loans, IRA, or my savings.

The best way to ensure that all of your bills are paid on time is to enroll in automatic payments with automatic bill pay. An automatic payment is when you have a payment of a bill be deducted from your account automatically every due date. You can set this up through the vendor or merchant you need to pay. Once you set it, then you can forget about worrying if the bill will be paid on time. You can also have bills be automatically paid to your credit card.

Automatic bill pay happens this way:
- The amount of a bill will be automatically deducted from your checking

account or charged to your credit card at the same time every month. In order to set this up, you must sign into the online account management site of whoever is billing you and use their system to set up automatic payment. This is what I do for my utilities, cell phone, and TV bills.

Online Bill Pay works this way:

• Sign into online banking with your financial institution and set up each bill as a payee. Once a month, you go in and set the payment date, save it, and let the bank take care of the rest. In this situation, you need the money in advance of the bill being paid. You will need enough money to be taken out of your account when the check is mailed, which has to be early enough for the company to receive it before the due date.

Having the bill paid automatically eliminates the possibility of you forgetting to pay the bill or paying late. In life, you have to be proactive and think ahead.

I use my credit card for most of my automatic payments so I can earn rewards faster. If you have to pay the bill anyway, might as well get rewards for doing so.

If you are afraid of automatic bill payment, then you need to devise your own method of reminding yourself to pay every bill on time each month. Here are a few ideas:

• Alerts from each vendor about due dates of bills via email
• Schedule an alarm on your cell phone or email calendar to remind yourself to pay each bill every month
• Written notes posted on the fridge
• Using a planner/ organizer

Cash Advances

Before agreeing to accept any credit card, you always want to look at the fine print. The fine print will tell you the real information regarding the interest rate, balance transfer rules, and any consequences associated with not paying. For example, if you want to transfer the balance of three different credit cards onto one card for one low monthly payment, you have the right idea, but check the fine print. I only recommend consolidating if it's a good deal and will save you money. Each balance transfer will probably cost you a 3-5% fee on the balance you transferred. Please note, you will be paying interest on this fee as well as the balance you transferred. Also, remember to include the transfer fee in your calculations for balance totals in relation to your credit limit. I would hate to have you be charged an over the limit fee because of a balance transfer fee.

While the fee isn't much, it's still more money that you eventually need to pay back. In certain situations the fee is a small price to pay for future savings. If you are consolidating credit from three other cards with interest rates of over 20%, and you are balance transferring the balances onto a card with 0% interest for the first six months then fixed at 9% thereafter, that ends up being monumental savings.

Cash advances and balance transfers always have a higher interest rate than regular purchases unless it is a special promotion. Towards the end of your statement, your financial institution should list the different transaction categories applied to your account. Look at the example below:

Finance Charge Schedule					
Category	Promotional Transaction Types	Daily Periodic Rate	Corresponding Annual Percentage Rate	APR Type	Balance Subject to Finance Charge
Balance Transfers		0.016438% V	6.0%	S	$0.00
Cash Advances		0.016438% V	6.0%	S	$609.44
Purchases		0.016438% V	6.0%	S	$0.00
Annual Percentage Rate for this Billing Period:					6.00%
(Includes Periodic Rate Finance Charges and Transaction Fee Finance Charges that results in a n APR which exceeds the Corresponding APR above.)					

APR Type Definitions: Daily Interest Rate Type: V= Variable Rate (Interest Rate may vary); APR Type : S= Standard APR (APR normally in effect)

On balance transfers: my daily period rate (daily interest rate) is .016438% and my APR (my actual interest rate) is 6%. The type of transaction is my Standard APR (not a special promotional APR) and I am currently paying interest for a balance transfer on a $0 balance.

Confused? My interest rate (or my APR) is 6% for every category of purchase. This is NOT common; I just happen to be lucky enough to have a good deal. My 6% APR is then broken down into a daily interest rate, which is .016438%. This daily interest rate is applied to my balance every day. When the interest is added up, I am charged a total of a .5% interest on my outstanding balance. How did I come up with .5%? Take the APR (the A stands for annual) and divide by 12, as in 12 months to a year.

Some banks, like mine, calls interest a finance charge. For most cases, finance charges and interest are the same.

I recommend having your credit card with the same financial institution as your checking and savings accounts. This allows you to easily make a payment on the card online, over the phone, at the ATM, or in a banking center.

Credit Unions

Credit unions are financial institutions that offer all of the same products as a traditional bank, but the accounts have an affect on your credit. To open an account at a credit union you must be affiliated with an organization or group that is a member of that union. If you aren't personally affiliated maybe your parents are, so check with them. Credit unions are great for people looking to rebuild their credit after a previous blunder or to begin their credit history.

There is no rule stating you must stay with only one bank at a time. If you enjoy the account you have at a certain bank, you don't need to close your account in order to get a credit union account. You are allowed to have multiple accounts. Just make sure you can handle it and can control your money responsibly. If you have an account with a financial institution and you truly enjoy their services, you don't need to leave them. Keep the majority of your funds with them, but open a savings account with the credit union to build your credit. Make sure you can afford to make regular deposits into this account, even if it's only $10.

Overdraft Protection

A credit card is the best option for overdraft protection if:

A) You don't keep money in a savings account or

B) You have a savings account with a different financial institution than where your checking account is.

I highly recommend banking all in one place, as this just makes gaining control of your finances much easier. I also recommend that you use a credit card for overdraft protection and not your savings. If you use your savings account for overdraft protection, you have to front the money and have it sitting there waiting to be used. If you don't have the money already there, you aren't protected because the bank won't overdraw your savings to prevent your checking from overdrawing. I would prefer you keep the bulk of all savings in an online account anyway so you earn more money.

With a credit card, you are protected by borrowed money, so if you are in a financial jam (which is usually the case when you overdraw), you can pay the money back later. If you really are strapped for cash, chances are you won't have too much money in the savings account to help if you were to overdraw. From my experiences, people generally have more credit available to them than money saved up

Consequences

As long as the credit card is open, active, and you pay on time, you are taking the first step to building healthy credit. A missed or late payment can ruin your credit standing, especially with the company you have the card with. A missed or late payment will not only affect your relationship with that particular financial institution, but it will also affect the APR and your relationship with your other creditors as well. Creditors constantly check on your credit to see how you are doing even after they have extended you credit. If you become a higher credit risk, these companies are going to position themselves to be protected by either raising your rates or asking for a security deposit from you.

Checking and savings accounts don't have an affect on your credit score. The only time a checking or savings account affects your credit is if you go delinquent on your account, bring it into the negative, and don't repay the overdue amount. If you do this, you will be submitted to ChexSystems.

If you have been submitted to ChexSystems, then it will be extremely difficult to open another checking or savings account with any other financial institution. Furthermore, it will be extremely difficult to get a credit card, a loan, or a mortgage. While you may not be thinking of getting a mortgage now, you might in four or five years. Being submitted to ChexSystems when you were younger can now affect you as an adult. Furthermore, once you are out of ChexSystems, you will have to start building your credit score from scratch. Refer to the checking chapter for information about ChexSystems.

10

Getting Out of Debt

IF YOU FIND YOURSELF IN EXTREME CREDIT CARD or other loan debt, don't worry; there are ways out! While you can go from debt free to maxed out overnight, getting out of debt isn't as easy. Try not to worry though, as there is always help available.

Be Debt Free

Here is a list of ways to get out of debt:

Cut back on excessive spending. I know this is a lot easier said than done, but you got yourself into this mess, so you need to take charge and get yourself out of it. Whenever you make a purchase, evaluate whether it is a need or a want. Stop buying things you don't *need*.

Keep making at least the minimum payment due on ALL of your credit accounts. Remember, your payment history accounts for 35% of your FICO credit score. The better your score, the better the interest rate will be. The better the interest rate, the lower the amount you pay in interest. If you have a good enough score, you can always apply for a new credit card with 0% interest for the first 6-12 months and balance transfer your cards all on to one card. Consolidating is essential in eliminating high interest.

Don't cancel your cards once you pay them off. Keep them open to improve your debt ratio. Once you get enough paid off, start closing the newest cards first. If you have a department store card or a credit card with an annual fee (and you don't use them/ they aren't beneficial to you) then close these out once you've paid them off.

If you are trying to pay off debt on a credit card, a way to show the bank you are making an effort is to pay more than double the minimum payment. This means, if your minimum payment is $50 a month, pay at least $101. Only making minimum payments on all accounts shows the bank that you may not be trying to get out of debt. Making more than double shows good faith and determination on your behalf.

<u>The Plan</u>

If you're in credit card debt, I recommend making a chart of all of your credit cards, coming up with a repayment plan, and sticking to it. You're going to need discipline to get yourself out of debt. I know it's not fun, but now that you own that brand new TV and the Xbox, you need to focus on paying off your new toys.

A credit card chart is something that will help visualize what your debt looks like. Use the following model for yourself.

Credit Card	Interest Rate	Balance	Credit Limit
Bank A Visa	18.9%	$2000	$2500
Bank B MasterCard	13%	$900	$1000
Dept. Store C Card	21%	$400	$700
Dept. Store D Card	0% for 6 Months, then 15%	$600	$800

This is not just an example that came out of nowhere. The example above is an exact replica of one of my best friends' finances. As you can see, at the point when he asked for my help, he was $3900 in credit card debt out of a possible $5,000. He was 78% in debt!

For this example and to preserve his identity, let's call my friend Eugene. Now Eugene budgeted $300 a month for credit card payments. After creating the chart, I told Eugene to pay off his Dept. Store C Card first because the interest rate is higher than any of the other cards. In deciding which card to pay off first, or which loan to pay off first, pay the card with the highest interest rate, not highest balance. The higher the interest rate, the more money you end up paying in interest, and the more compounding negatively affects you.

Now, just because Eugene needs to focus on one card doesn't mean he can forget about his other cards. He needs to pay the minimum due on the other three cards, and then put the remainder of the budgeted $300 towards the Dept. Store C Card. For the sake of our example, let's say that the minimum payment due is $20. After one month, this is what Eugene's chart looks like:

Credit Card	Interest Rate	Balance	Credit Limit
Bank A Visa	18.9%	2011.19	2500
Bank B MasterCard	13%	889.53	1000
Dept. Store C Card	21%	162.80	700
Dept. Store D Card	0% for 6 Months, then 15%	580	800

So, $20 went to the Bank A Visa, Bank B MasterCard, and Dept. Store D Card. $240 went to the Dept. Store C Card. Assuming no other charges were placed on the cards (except for interest), Eugene brought his debt ratio down from 78% to 73%. While just a small change right now, it's a lot better than the ratio going up. If Eugene keeps up this payment plan, he will be able to pay off the Dept. Store C Card in just one more month, then start making a dent into his huge Visa bill. Also, after each card gets paid off, you are able to make bigger payments on the card you are focusing on next. After the Dept. Store C Card is paid off, Eugene will be able to make a $260 payment per month towards his Bank A Visa bill.

Once Eugene pays off the Dept. Store C Card, he needs to keep it open, unless he is being charged a maintenance fee. You should never keep a credit card that charges you fees just for having it. When Eugene asked for my help he was $3900 in debt out of a possible $5000, or 78% in debt. Closing out the Dept. Store C Card, while still having the other cards stay the same would bring him to $3300 in debt out of a possible $4300, which is 77%, not a good improvement from before. If he keeps the Dept. Store C Card open however, he will be 66% in debt. That's a 12-point improvement! Why is this so important? 30% of your credit score is based on your credit/ debt ratio.

Eugene stuck to his repayment plan and cut out excessive spending. He picked up extra shifts at work when he could and evaluated what he bought. Was it a want or a need? He said it "really sucked" but he's glad he did it.

<u>Quick pointers on credit cards:</u>

Now I know you may think I am crazy, but I'm not. Closing out a credit card hurts your credit score because you're eliminating a part of your credit history. If you have too many cards, you are invariably hurting your score with fiscal irresponsibility. A little dip now in your credit score when you're young won't hurt you for too long, and will help you in the long run.

• You want to keep the cards that you have had the longest open because it shows longevity in your credit report and makes up 35% of your credit score. You would only want to close out the card you have had the longest if there is something fundamentally wrong with it (a really high interest rate or an annual fee) or if it's a department store credit card.

• Store/department store credit cards generally have high interest rates and hidden fees. I recommend not having them unless this is the only way you can get a credit card. If that is the case, then get one, use it, build a credit history and get a regular credit card ASAP. If you have a store credit card, keep it only if you shop there often, the rewards you receive are worth it to you, and you pay your balance in full every month.

• Banking all in one place is the easiest way to bank. If you are torn between two cards and don't know which card to keep open, I recommend keeping the credit card with your current financial institution open. Having your credit card in the same place as your checking makes it easier to make payments and service your account.

• As you close out your cards, call the credit card company who owns the card you plan on keeping and ask them to increase your limit, as this will keep your ratio in check. Your creditors may not do this, so keep that in mind. I am not telling you to increase your limit so you can get into even more financial trouble. If having more credit available to you would tempt you, then don't do it. Remember, we are working to better your financial foundation, not crack it even more.

• Try to consolidate your debt if possible. If you have bad credit, you may not be getting good deals when you consolidate. Consolidating just to consolidate isn't wise; you should only do so when a good opportunity presents itself. You can either transfer balances onto a card you already have (if the bank is offering you to do so at a low rate) or you can apply for a new card. New cards generally have a promotion, which will offer 0% or a low interest rate for the first six to twelve months of the card being opened, then a somewhat higher interest rate afterwards. Consider using that six to twelve months of no interest to pay off your debts and not rack up more.

If you can't get a new card, call your financial institution and ask them to lower your interest rate. Financial institutions don't want to lose you as a customer, so if you tell them you are thinking of closing out your account, they might make a deal. Tell them it's because the interest rate is too high and that a competitor has offered you a better deal (even if they haven't); they might lower your rate to get you to stay. Remember, banks make millions of dollars a year on interest off of their customers; they don't want to lose you. Also, it doesn't hurt to ask. Worse thing they can say is "no."

FICO Score

When applying for a credit card or any line of credit, companies check your credit report and your FICO credit score. Your credit report contains important information about your credit history. Here is what your FICO score is made up of:

35% of Score	30% of Score	15% of Score	10% of Score	10% of Score
Bill Payment History	Debt to Credit Ratio	Longevity	Recent Credit Applications and Accounts	Variety of Credit Accounts
The pattern of paying your bills on time.	How much you owe in debt compared to total amount of credit available. Remember, the lower the better.	How long you have had a credit history. Hopefully you started when you turned 18!	If you just got a credit card, why do you need another one?	Do you have just credit cards? Or do you have loans and bills in your name too? Variety of accounts shows responsibility.

Free Credit Reports

It is in your benefit to check your credit report often. Why? Because checking your credit report allows you to be in control of your finances and be proactive in keeping your financial record clean. Checking your credit report will alert you to any mistakes (such as an account that is shown as open, but should have been closed) and to possible identity theft (were *you* the one who opened that mortgage on the other side of the country?)

The following are the web addresses of the three credit bureaus:
http://www.experian.com/
http://www.transunion.com/
http://www.equifax.com/

Per federal law, you are allowed to view your credit report for free (and with no mark against your credit) once a year from each major credit bureau (Equifax, TransUnion, Experian). Go to https://www.annualcreditreport.com to get your free credit report or to get more information. You do not get your credit score with your credit report; it will cost you extra to see that, after all, these credit bureaus need to make money somehow, right?

A person's credit report can be checked one of two ways:

1. Some people want to check their credit just once a year and get all three free credit reports at once. This way you can see what each credit bureau has marked on your credit. Major companies will report credit information to all 3 bureaus, whereas smaller companies may only report to one. This could mean, what is on one credit report, may not be on the others. Seeing all at once allows you to compare and contrast.

2. Others get one free credit report every four months, this way they are always checking in on their credit report. This is what I do. Since all of my credit accounts are with big companies, I know they all report the same information to all 3 bureaus. So, for the most part, my credit report will be the same from report to report.

Look at all of the information on your credit thoroughly. If you find any discrepancy on one your credit reports, you need to contact all of the credit bureaus immediately.

Time is your friend in building a healthy credit history and a strong credit score. Start early, be responsible, and you will be golden. Think carefully before you close any credit account in your name. If the card is detrimental, then by all means close it, but if you have had a card for years, and there are no fees, then keep the account open. Longevity works to your advantage in the world of credit. Close problematic and newer cards first if you do close

out a credit account. And when you do close out a credit account, see if you can increase your credit limit on another card to keep your debt ratio low.

If you are at a point where debt is consuming your life, speak to your financial institution and they can help you. Your financial institution can work with you to set up a payment schedule to help you pay back your debt.

Credit card companies will work with you in order to get their money. The flexibility of repayment terms depends on your standing with the financial institution.

If talking directly to your credit card company doesn't work, there are debt management companies out there who can help you get your life back on track, for a small fee of course.

One final note about loans and credit cards, I highly recommend that you not overpay. For example, if you have a credit card balance of $100, don't make a payment for $150. Yes, you will probably spend that $50 eventually but until you do, why would you loan the bank that money interest free? The bank won't pay you interest on the money you over paid but they will certainly use it to make themselves more money.

11

Tying It All Together

I know that's a lot of information, theory and knowledge. In this section I will tie it all in together. I'll show you how it's applied in real life and how you can apply it in your life. This section is dedicated to how I apply all of this information in my own life.

All Together Now

What I Currently Have:

    1 traditional checking account
    1 traditional savings account
    1 credit card with a really low APR I use for overdraft protection I've had since I turned 18
    1 online savings account
    1 Business Credit Card through American Express

1 airlines personal credit card through American Express

2 IRAs- One that is aggressive and one that is a LifePath Fund managed to be as profitable as it can be until I go to retire.

1 investment account

1 Federally Subsidized Stafford Student Loan

1 Private Education Loan

1 iPhone plan with 450 minutes, unlimited text and data

I have one checking account where all of my money is deposited into then transferred to the appropriate place. My online savings account is where I put the bulk of my savings. My traditional savings account is where I keep money for bills for the month.

I will always keep my traditional credit card with the really low APR that I've had since I was 18. Longevity is crucial in determining your credit score and the low APR helps me save money on interest..

My business credit card keeps all of my business purchases separate from my personal spending.

My airline credit card is used for personal expenses while earning airline miles, which I use when traveling to film festivals and vacation. My other personal credit card is used strictly for overdraft protection.

Every month I contribute to my two IRA's with an automatic deduction from my checking account. This makes sure that I am saving money for my retirement. Since I contribute the same amount every month (dollar cost averaging) some months I get more shares of the mutual fund I am invested in than others, as it's based on the fund price on the day of the contribution. The law of averages says that, overall, this method will be most beneficial for people. While some months you may only get a few shares, the next month you might get more. You don't want to only contribute when the stock price is low because then you won't have as many shares at the end of the year than you would if you just contributed every month.

I recently had a 401(k) until I transferred it into one of my existing IRAs.

My investment account started after I redeemed all of the savings bonds I had been given as a child. There is a bigger potential for returns on the stock market than in a fixed rate bond. I took the money and invested in a few companies I am passionate about and think will do well.

My federally subsidized Stafford loan is automatically deducted from my checking account every month. The federal government provides this loan and every student who fills out the FAFSA is eligible. The maximum of what you are lent increases for every year you are in college. This loan helps pay for college, has a fixed interest rate, and while you're in school there are no payments or interest accrued. Because the federal government guarantees the loan, every financial institution offers this type of loan. What it means when I say that the federal government guarantees the loan is that the government guarantees it will be paid. If, in a freak accident, you pass away, the government will repay your debt to the bank in full. So, for banks, there is no risk of not getting paid back.

My first year of college student loan was through Sallie Mae. After significantly paying the balance down, I balance transferred the loan to a credit card because of the significant drop in the interest rate. CAUTION- this isn't the best choice for everyone. If you lose your job or are unable to pay your bill, you have fewer options in lowering your payment or potentially deferring payment or getting a forbearance if it's a credit card instead of an educational loan.

My second year of college loan was through Wachovia but then became Wells Fargo. Auto payment is set up through Wells Fargo so I can get a slight reduction in my interest rate on the loan. Such a small change will save me hundreds of dollars in future interest. Because I have a lot of bills every month, I am on a graduated repayment plan with this loan. Meaning, right now I have a lower monthly payment, but in a few years the minimum payment will increase. Hopefully, in the future I'll be able to better afford paying the loan back. For me, I know this to be true, as I will have my car and my first year loan paid off within a year. I can then take the funds from my budget for those payments and switch it to paying this loan.

What I Do:
If I am being paid via Direct Deposit I split my paycheck between my checking account and my online savings account. It's important to pay myself first, so I make sure that I deposit 10% of my paycheck into my savings account. The rest of my paycheck is deposited into my checking account.

If I am being paid with an actual check, I just deposit the check into my regular savings account until I have enough or more than enough to pay for my bills, then I start depositing the checks into my checking account.

I do this for every paycheck, starting at the beginning of the month, until there is enough money in my regular savings account to pay for all of my bills for that month. If the money is going to sit there for 20 days, might as well earn some interest on it, right? I make sure that there is always enough money in the regular savings account to pay for: rent, gas/electric, cable/internet, student loan payments and credit card minimum payments.

Now, most of my automatic payments happen at around the same time every month. So, before the payments for the month start coming out, I do one transfer from my savings to my checking. This prevents me from getting charged for too many withdrawals.

What's left over is mine to spend. What I end up doing is use my rewards credit card for every purchase I make, then make one payment to that credit card at the end of the month to pay it off. This way I am earning rewards or cash back on a purchase I was going to make anyway (food, entertainment, etc.)

How do I not overspend? The simple and un-fun answer is discipline and sacrifice. I am always aware of how much money is in my checking account and what I've already purchased. If I decide to go out with friends, I figure out what works for my budget on how much I can spend and I stick to it. I don't go over and I try to spend less if I can. I also manage when I do things. If I've gone out twice this week, I'll have to pass on a third or fourth so I can stick to my budget.

Certain expenses that occur every month have an affect on your credit. When you rent an apartment or house, the landlord checks your credit. When you apply for cell phone service, the provider checks your credit. When you get cable or Internet, the provider checks your credit. Not only do these places check your credit, but also they report your repayment history to the credit bureaus. That's why I automatically pay everything from my checking account or credit card. No opportunity to miss out on paying something and hurting my credit. If the company providing you a service needs your social security number in order to provide that service to you, they will check and then report on, your credit. Don't give them any excuse to put a bad mark on there. Because of my good credit, I've been able to get my own apartment without needing my parents as co-signers. I've been able to get good deals and offers on credit cards, which I then use to pay off student loans or other debt I have at low or no interest.

Getting a Car

How did I manage to buy a car? Good question. My first car was purchased in high school. I had saved money up from when I was younger and luckily had enough savings to buy a used car from my cousin. I knew the car was in good condition because my family takes extra good care of their vehicles. Because I was family I was also given a good deal. When I moved to NYC I sold my car and put the money in my savings account.

Over the course of five years in NYC I used my savings to help me survive, but I also kept adding money to it. Because, at least in my mind, you never know when you'll need the money. When I recently moved from NYC to LA I was able to afford a used car by paying for it partially through my savings and partially by balance transferring the remaining balance onto one of my credit cards with a 0% interest rate for 18 months. Since what I owe on my car is on a credit card that has become my "car payment." I make monthly payments of $250 on the credit card even though the minimum monthly payment is much lower. If I keep paying that amount every month, I'll have the car paid off well before the 18 months is over.

In preparation for buying a car I saved, saved, saved. Any left over money, any work bonus, any holiday or birthday money I got, went straight to my savings.

Getting a Student Loan

In preparation for going to college I started a conversation with my financial aid department at my school. I auditioned for scholarship money and spoke to them on ways to afford attending school. I had to fill out the FAFSA (Free Application for Federal Student Aid) in order to get student loans. After the FAFSA determined that my parents made too much money for me to get any kind of federal help going to school, I opted to get a Federally Subsidized Stafford Loan. This loan is a small loan and didn't come close to covering my total college expenses. So, I started looking for student loan providers to get a private education loan. I spoke to my college to see which loan providers they worked with on a regular basis to make the process easier. They gave me some recommendations and that's whom I went with.

Even though my parents weren't helping me pay for college, I still had to use their information for my FAFSA. You no longer have to use your parents' incomes for the FAFSA when you are either married or turn 24. Once I had to start applying for private loans (roughly $58,000 in loans) I convinced my parents to co-sign the loan with me. I may have good credit, but not THAT good. A college student doesn't make enough money for a bank to loan them such a substantial amount. After convincing my parents to co-sign, I had to start making payments on the loan. My parents may have co-signed, but they weren't going to make any payments.

Though I didn't legally have to make payments until after I graduated (repayment on student loans begin six months after graduation) my parents said a condition of them co-signing was immediate repayment of the loan. So, even though I was in school 50 plus hours a week, I continued to work in order to make payments while in school. $220 (at least) every month was paid to my loan. This amount came from a $200 a month payment, plus $200 split over 12 months to essentially make 13 payments every 12 months. I rounded up to the nearest $10 mark, thus creating my $220 a month payment.

Getting an Apartment

When I had to move out of the dorms, I immediately lived with a friend who already had an apartment. For roughly 6 months I was a roommate or subletting in a location where I wasn't on the lease. Once I had saved up enough money I moved out on my own. I had saved enough money to pay for the first and last months rent and a hefty security deposit. Since I had never had a lease in my name and I didn't make 80 times the monthly rent (NYC apartments are EXPENSIVE) I was able to make a deal with them to let me rent there if I fronted a substantial amount of money. I did this for my next two apartments until I was able to find roommates who also had good enough credit where we were all on the lease together.

Odds and Ends

If you notice an error on your account, try to remain calm. I cannot tell you how many times people come in to a banking center, yelling and screaming at a teller for an error on their account. First of all, it most likely was not that individual teller's fault that there is an error on your account. Secondly, nobody wants to deal with an irrational customer. You need to breathe, come in, and be calm and understanding. The bank will do everything in their power to rectify the situation. The bank needs you and your money. Yelling gets you nowhere in a banking center or with customer service over the phone.

This should go without saying, but you should never degrade a bank associate, or anyone for that matter. They are there to do a job. They do not have a personal vendetta against you; so don't have one against them. Nobody should have to deal with being insulted at his or her job. The teller doesn't do that to you at your job, so please provide the same courtesy to them. Furthermore, a bank associate will work harder to rectify the situation for you when you are pleasant and calm as opposed to being obnoxious. Why would someone spend their time helping someone who is cruel and mean when they could be using that same time to help other customers who are pleasant?

If you notice an error on your account, or you notice a fraudulent charge pending on your account, you need to wait until this questionable charge actually posts to your account. Banks can only start to rectify the situation once the charge has posted to your account. If it's just pending, there is a possibility it won't post, which is why banks only investigate fraudulent charges once they actually post to your account.

Always keep a keen eye on your accounts, both depository and credit. If you notice a discrepancy then take care of it immediately. The earlier you discover the mistake, the easier it can be amended. Your credit report and monthly statements should be reviewed often.

Keep all of your receipts as proof of every purchase. Once you receive your monthly statement, cross-reference your statement with your handwritten register. If there is a discrepancy, you have your receipts as proof. Every statement cycle, shred old receipts and paper statements. Checking your credit report will help you make sure there aren't random accounts opened under your name and also help you make sure any old credit accounts are actually closed. If there is any discrepancy, you need to contact the credit bureaus immediately.

When I was a teller, some people just wouldn't listen to what I had to say, even if I wasn't trying to sell them anything. For example, a person can reorder checks online, instead of coming into a banking center. If I tried to do my job and tell that person how they can reorder the checks online, his or her response is invariably "I'm not interested". Not interested in what? I wasn't asking for you to be interested in anything, I was simply informing you. In essence, treat others how you would like to be treated.

In the world of smart phones, there are many apps out there to help you stay on top of your financial game. My personal favorites are Check (formerly Pageonce) and Credit Karma. Check (formerly Pageonce) allows you to have one interface where you can see all of your bills, depository accounts and investment accounts at one. Credit Karma is an amazing app that helps you stay on top of your credit score and gives you hints on how to improve your score.

That's a Wrap!

Well folks, that's a wrap. I have imparted my wisdom to the best of my ability and now I leave it up to you. What you do with the knowledge is up to you, but I hope you take what I have written and apply it to your lives. I am tired of people thinking our generation is lazy and unmotivated. Now is our opportunity to show them that we are intelligent and we can handle being adults. After all, we are the future of this world.

I would love to hear your feedback, so please find me online and let me know how you feel about my book. Visit me online at www.stoc.biz.

12
Common Terms

Throughout this book, I've mentioned many things particular to banks, banking, financial planning and debt. To some extent I defined them as I went. Just in case though, I've included the following glossary of terms to help you figure out what some of the most common items and expressions are and mean as you deal with the banking and financial world.

401(k)- Employer sponsored retirement account. A retirement account you deposit money into on a pre-tax basis with every paycheck. Most employers will match your contributions up to a certain percent. You can only deposit money into these types of accounts while employed. If you leave that job, you can no longer make new deposits to the account.

Account Number- A sequence of numbers that designates your account from another person's account. Only your account will have your account number.

Account Servicing- A banking term which means any change to your account. These services include: changing address/ phone number, the fee structure, re-ordering checks or deposit slips, setting up an automatic transfer, ordering a new debit card, changing your pin number, etc.

ACH- Automated Clearing House. The ACH is the electronic network your direct deposit, automatic payments and credit and debit purchases are processed through. According to the dictionary: "an electronic clearing and settlement system for electronic financial transactions among participating US commercial banks and depository institutions."

APR- Annual Percentage Rate. The interest rate for your loan or savings account that will be applied to your account over the course of a year.
APY- Annual Percentage Yield. The interest rate for your loan or savings account after you factor in compound interest over the course of a year.

Automatic Payment- A recurring payment that you set up to be paid automatically, without your intervention, once you set it up. My recommendation of how you should pay all bills.

Available Balance- The funds that are available in your account to you to use.

Blank Check- A check with just your account number on it and no identifiable or supplemental information. A small number of blank checks are generally given to you when you open a new account. Once you're account is opened, banks are unable to give you blank checks later, generally.

Business Day- Any day falling between Monday and Friday that is not a federal holiday.

Cash Back- When doing a purchase, asking the cashier to charge you an extra amount (for example, $20) and then getting that extra charge back to you in cash. Cash back can only be done on debit purchases and not credit purchases.

Cashier's Check- A certified check created by a bank employee which is paid for in advance. These checks are guaranteed funds. Generally you must purchase a cashier's check for a small fee.

CD- A Certificate of Deposit. This is an FDIC-insured, low-risk investment. You are essentially loaning the financial institution your money in return for a fixed interest rate and return. Since you have no access to your funds during this time, your interest rate is higher than a savings account.

CD Term- The length of time the bank will hold your money.

Check 21 Law- A federal law passed in 2006 which allows banks to process transactions involving checks faster. Essentially, instead of the receiving financial institution sending the physical check itself to the bank where the check is from, financial institutions are allowed to send electronic copies of the check, speeding up processing times drastically.

Checking Account- a type of depository account where multiple debits and credits are allowed for no fee. Checks can be written out of these accounts and are the staple to any person who deals with money.

ChexSystems^{SM} – A database comprised of member Financial Institutions that regularly contribute information on mishandled checking and savings accounts. ChexSystems shares this information among member institutions to help them assess the risk of opening new accounts.

Co-Branded Credit Card- A credit card that is offered by a financial institution in conjunction with a charity or business who is not the financial institution. Their rewards program is geared towards rewarding the consumer with that business' products. Examples include charity credit cards that donate money to a charity or cause, or an airline credit card where points are redeemed for flights.

Completely Free Account- An account with no monthly maintenance fee. No balance requirements or direct deposit requirements. Does not exclude you from being assessed an overdraft fee.

Compound Interest- Interest paid on both the principal and on accrued interest.

Compromised Account Number- When an unauthorized and potential dangerous third party gains access to your account number for fraudulent use.

Credit Union- A financial institution that helps you build your credit with depository and loan accounts when you have accounts in good standing with them. Accounts are only available to its membership through specific organizations.

Credits- The name for transactions that positively affect your balance on your accounts. Credits include payments to a credit account or deposits to a checking account.

Current Balance- Your balance on an account at the beginning of that business day after everything from the previous business day has posted to your account. Excludes any pending purchases or deposits made on that business day. Also, your current balance is the balance used to base authorizations for purchases off of.

Customer Service Requests- See Account Servicing.

Debits- The name for transactions that negatively affect your balance on your accounts. Debits include purchases and bill payments.

Default [on a loan]- When you fail to make payments on a loan.

Depository Account- An account where you can access the funds quickly and make regular deposits into. It is not an investment account. (A Checking or Savings account).

Direct Deposit- When you get paid electronically. Instead of receiving a check, the payer sends the money to your account through the Automated Clearing House. Funds are always guaranteed with direct deposits, which means, the check will never come back for insufficient funds. According to the dictionary: "a plan in which salaries or other payments are transferred by the paying agency directly to the accounts of the recipients."

Endorse (Endorsing a Check)- When you sign the back of a check. Signing the back of the check means you are taking responsibility for the check you're presenting to the bank. You must endorse a check in order to collect the funds.

FAFSA (Free Application of Federal Student Aid)- The application for federal financial assistance. This must be filled out in order to obtain any kind of educational loan. A student must use their parent's financial statistics as part of the application until the student is married or turns 24. www.fafsa. ed.gov

FDIC- Federal Depositors Insurance Company. An independent agency of the United States government that protects you (the consumer) against the loss of your deposits if an FDIC-insured bank or savings association fails.

Essentially, they are the insurance company that makes sure you don't lose your money if your bank goes bankrupt.

FDIC Insured- A classification for depository accounts. If your bank is a member of the FDIC, all depository accounts are FDIC insured. So, if that institution fails or goes bankrupt, you won't lose your money, up to $250,000. Investment accounts are NOT insured, because investments are based off of the stock market, which is not guaranteed.

Federally Subsidized Stafford Loans- A student loan that is offered by a bank and backed and guaranteed by the federal government. The bank has no risk in offering this loan to you, because if you were to die, the government would then pay the remainder of your loan. If you default on the loan, it will negatively affect your credit. Also, while you are in school, the government pays the interest on the loan. There are limits on how much money in Subsidized Stafford loans you can get per year and repayment begins six months after graduation.

Federally Unsubsidized Stafford Loans- If you qualify, after you max out your subsidized Stafford loan amount per school year, you can apply for more federal government money to pay for college. The interest rate should be the same as the subsidized Stafford loan. You are responsible for paying the interest accrued while you are in school and repayment begins six months after graduation.

Fund Availability- The schedule of when the funds you deposited will be available for you to use. Fund availability is instantaneous for direct deposits and cash deposits. Check deposit fund availability range from instantaneous to up to ten business days.

Funds- Money.

Future Dating a Check- When you put a date on the check you are writing for some point in the future. Banks are not supposed to process a check until the date on the check has occurred.

Gross Pay- What you make at your job based on your wage before taxes are taken out.

Guaranteed Funds- When the money is guaranteed to be there when it is presented for deposit or to be cashed. Direct deposits, money orders and cashier's checks are all examples of transactions where the funds are guaranteed. Money orders and cashiers checks are guaranteed because they are paid for up front.

Hold- A delay of fund availability based on your relationship with the financial institution. Funds can be delayed for 1 to 10 business days. Different banks have different criteria for why a hold is placed. What is able to be held and for how long is governed by federal banking law known as Reg CC. Cash is available immediately.

Instant Gratification- The notion of not working for or waiting to get something you want. Instead of planning and saving to purchase or get something, it's the ability to charge the purchase to a credit card, get the product right then and there, and worry about paying it back later.

In-State Deposit- When a deposit occurs within the state in which the account was originally opened.

Interest- Money charged (if a credit/loan account) or earned (if a savings account) on an account based on the balance of the account.

IRA- Individual Retirement Account. This is your self-sponsored 401(k). A retirement account that you can deposit money into whenever you want, and is not based on employment requirements. There is a maximum yearly limit. The limit in 2010 was $5,000. IRAs can be either Traditional or Roth. The basic difference is when you withdraw funds from a Traditional IRA you pay taxes on that money. A Roth IRA grows tax differed and you don't pay taxes when you do withdrawals. When you deposit into a Traditional IRA you can take a deduction on that year's tax returns, while you cannot do that for a Roth IRA.

Less Cash Deposit- When you are depositing a check, but want some money back from that check. A less cash deposit is a type of deposit where you can accomplish both transactions in one.

Liquidity- How quickly you can turn an asset into cash.

Live Check- A check that hasn't been processed or liquidated yet, and the date of the check is either that day or has passed. Essentially, a live check is a check that is able to be negotiated.

Maturity Date- When a CD term ends and you are able to reclaim your money and interest.

MICR- Stands for Magnetic Ink Character Recognition. The series of numbers on the bottom of all checks. The MICR line is written in special ink that contains magnetic particles which banks use as a security measure. If a check's MICR line isn't written in MICR ink, the check cannot be scanned by a MICR reader, which can aid in discovering if the check is fraudulent.

The routing number, account number and check number make up the MICR line.

Money Order- A certified document created by a bank employee which is paid for in advance. These are guaranteed funds that you purchase for a small fee. The US Post Office also sells money orders.

Negotiate- The ability to use a check as legal tender (money). If a check isn't filled out properly, then the teller cannot use that check as money, and therefore cannot honor your check. Cash is negotiated regularly as legal tender. Negotiating a check is in essence an exchange; you exchange the check for the amount it is for, either in cash or for credit in your account. The Oxford dictionary defines "negotiate" (in terms of finances) as converting [a check, etc.] into money.

Net Pay- Also coined as "Take Home Pay," it's what you actually get to deposit into your account. It's the amount of money you earn at your job after taxes and other deductions are taken from your paycheck.

Non-Business Day- Any federal holiday that lands during a day Monday – Friday and the weekend, Saturday and Sunday.

Online Banking- A website owned, managed and operated by your financial institution. It's banking on the internet where you can complete simple transactions, such as transfers, bill payments, change of address and credit increase requests.

Out-of-State Deposit- A deposit taking place in a state other than the one the account was originally opened in.

Overdraft Protection- A bank program that transfers available money from either a depository or credit account to an account that is in danger of becoming overdrawn, thus preventing you from being charged an overdraft fee.

Parent PLUS Loans- The parental equivalent to the Federally Subsidized Stafford Loan. It's a loan your parents take out for you and your education. The maximum amount you can take out per year is drastically higher than the Federally Subsidized Stafford loan. Banks have less risk in offering these loans compared to a private education loan, because if your parents die before the loan is repaid, the government will pay off the loan. Your parents start repayment on these loans immediately and must pay the interest.

Payback Period- The length of time the bank plans on you to take to repay a loan. 30 Year mortgages have a 30 year payback period, meaning it would take that individual 30 years to completely pay the loan off. Payback periods for student loans generally last about 10 years. The payback period influences what makes up your minimum monthly payment. The longer the period the lower the monthly payment, but the more you end up paying in interest.

Posting- The process of finalizing a transaction on your account. Once something posts, the money has officially either been taken out or added to your account. You cannot dispute a charge on your account until it posts.

Principal- The amount/ balance of a loan or savings. This amount is the amount used to determine the interest that accrues on the account.

Regular Credit Card- A credit card offered strictly by a financial institution and not in conjunction with a charity or business. A regular credit card, as well as a co-branded credit card, are both unsecured loans, which means the bank is taking a risk by offering you credit. Most regular credit cards offer a simple rewards program.

Routing Number- A series of numbers that signify which state and which financial institution a certain account number belongs to.

Secured Credit Card- A credit card where you put down a security deposit first. Then, that security deposit is your credit limit. If you don't pay your credit card bill or you are late on your payment, the financial institution uses your full security deposit to repay your debt. There is no risk associated with offering a secured credit card since the security deposit guarantees the bank won't lose money.

Starter Checks- The initial set of checks you get when you open a new checking account. These checks are to allow you check access on your account while your check order arrives in the mail. After you use these blank checks, you cannot get more.

Stop Payment- A process of stopping payment on a check you wrote is to prevent the bank from paying that check. Generally, there is a fee associated with placing a stop payment on a check. It must be placed before the check is negotiated.

Straight Deposit- When you just deposit cash, check or both into your account with no cash back.

Target Date Mutual Fund- A type of mutual fund you invest in within your IRA or 401(k) that is professionally managed and diversified by the financial institution you opened your investment account with. These funds' goal is to maximize your investment by diversifying your investment and being high in risk while you are young and automatically rebalancing and becoming more conservative as you reach the target date (your desired age of retirement). Generally, it will be professionally managed for up to thirty years after it reaches its target date.

Third Party Check- A check that is trying to be negotiated by a person who is not the payee or the payer.

Traditional Financial Institution- A bank that is not a credit union, where their accounts do not have an effect on your credit.

Voided Check- A check with the word "VOID" written on it. Used to process a direct deposit request.

W4- A tax document given to your employer detailing how much in taxes should be taken out of your paycheck.

About the Author

STEVEN TYLOR O'CONNOR is an entertainment professional living in Los Angeles who grew up in Scottsdale, AZ. Working for Bank of America in high school, he started off as a teller and eventually became a Senior Teller trained as a Teller Operations Specialist.

As a young adult living in America right now, Steven has a first hand look into the daily trials and tribulations facing today's youth. With his experience, Steven can provide quality advice and tools to his peers to help them make sound financial decisions. Young adults generally don't have peers who know about finances. This book changes that.

To find out more information about Steven, visit his website at http://www.stoc.biz.